Indo-Malay Martial Traditions

Aesthetics, Mysticism, & Combatives

Vol. 2

An Anthology of Articles from the *Journal of Asian Martial Arts*

Edited by Michael A. DeMarco, M.A.

Disclaimer

Please note that the authors and publisher of this book are not responsible in any manner whatso-ever for any injury that may result from practicing the techniques and/or following the instructions given within. Since the physical activities described herein may be too strenuous in nature for some readers to engage in safely, it is essential that a physician be consulted prior to training.

All Rights Reserved

No part of this publication, including illustrations, may be reproduced or utilized in any form or by any means, electronic or mechanical, including photocopying, recording, or by any information storage and retrieval system (beyond that copying permitted by sections 107 and 108 of the US Copyright Law and except by reviewers for the public press), without written permission from Via Media Publishing Company.

Warning: Any unauthorized act in relation to a copyright work may result in both a civil claim for damages and criminal prosecution.

Copyright © 2015 by
Via Media Publishing Company
941 Calle Mejia #822
Santa Fe, NM 87501 USA
E-mail: md@goviamedia.com

All articles in this anthology were originally published in the *Journal of Asian Martial Arts*. Listed according to the table of contents for this anthology:

Pauka, K. (1997)	Volume 6, Number 1	pages 62–79
Pauka, K. (1997)	Volume 6, Number 4	pages 10–29
Pauka, K. (1997)	Volume 12, Number 1	pages 48–65
Wiley, M. (1993)	Volume 2, Number 4	pages 76–95
DeMarco, M. (1993)	Volume 19, Number 3	pages 96–113
Parker, C. (1995)	Volume 4, Number 4	pages 84–101

Book and cover design by Via Media Publishing Company

Edited by Michael A. DeMarco, M.A.

Cover illustration

Artwork © Pop Vichaya
Facebook.com/Pop315Photography

ISBN: 978-1893765-22-1

contents

preface

There seem to be more martial art styles in Southeast Asia than the number of islands in the region—and the Indonesian archipelago alone has 18,307 islands. We really don't know how many forms of silat are presently being practiced in Indonesia and Malaysia. Many arts are kept private, taught in secluded areas away from the public. These are arts of the older tradition, developed when combative knowledge was valued for its use in protecting the sanctity of life.

Popular martial arts in the Indo-Malay area reflect modern perspectives and interests, often exuding a competitive sport climate or simply serving as forms of athletic and aesthetic display. Taekwondo is one such popular art. But this two-volume anthology brings together a great collection of writings by authors who dive into the deepest realms of Indo-Malay combatives. They offer readers a rare viewing of martial traditions that is usually hidden behind social shrouds of secrecy and a clannish quest to preserve individual tradition.

A special presentation in this second volume are the writings of Dr. Kirstin Pauka forming three chapters on silat of West Sumatra, called *silek* in the Minangkabau language. The lead chapter discusses silek history, styles, training methods, and its use in dance. Martial arts in Indonesia often play a leading role in formal theatrical performances that take place to tell a story and reinforce traditional values. In chapter 2, Dr. Pauka shows that the martial arts constitute the core of the movement repertoire of the Randai folk theatre. Her third piece reports on an extended silek artist-in-residence program in the Asian Theatre program at the University of Hawai'i.

The next three chapters contains some academic coverage of kuntao-silat in the Indo-Malay traditions, garnished with technical sections illustrating the martial aspects of the arts. Mark Wiley details Silat Seni Gayong's ethical foundation for self-defense and nine techniqes illustrating the art with the help of Master Shiekh Shamsuddin.

My own chapter offers a glimpse of how cultural streams from India and China contributed over centuries to native Indonesian fighting arts to form hybrid systems. Examples were derived from personal observations of practitioners in the Willem Reeders lineage. The research shows the original intent and practices of any highly efficient combative art.

Chris Parker's insightful chapter discusses applications of specific movements, the rhythm that can be achieved when employing them, and the space they fill as being of crucial importance for defense. Pencak silat postures form the focus of this study.

All who are serious about the history and practice of Indo-Malay fighting arts will enjoy this special anthology, volumes 1 and 2. We are very fortunate to assemble the works of these highly qualified authors. Each chapter is a gem. We hope reading will provide information you seek. Although true silat masters are nearly impossible to find, the chapters here will certainly add direction and inspiration for practitioners.

Michael A. DeMarco
Santa Fe, New Mexico
November 2015

author bio notes

Michael A. DeMarco, M.A., received his degree from Seton Hall University's Asian Studies Department. In 1964 he began studies of Chinese-Indonesian kuntao-silat in the Willem Reeders tradition, primarily under Art Sikes, Thomas Pepperman, and Richard Lopez. Since 1973 he has focused on taijiquan: Yang style, Xiong Yanghe lineage; Chen style, Du Yuze lineage. He founded Via Media Publishing Company in 1991, producing the *Journal of Asian Martial Arts* and books. He teaches in Santa Fe, New Mexico.

Chris Parker, B.Ed., began training in Shotokan karate in 1973. After meeting silat teacher Bapak Hj Idris bin Alimuda in Cheltenham in 1976, he became a lifelong student. He is a licensed master practitioner of neuro linguistic programming and a highly experienced management trainer, business consultant, lecturer, and writer. Parker has been teaching the unique Malaysian style his teacher named Silat Fitrah. He is a lecturer in Sport & Leisure Management at Nottingham Trent University in the UK.

Kirstin Pauka, Ph.D., received her degree from Justus Liebig Universität in Germany and is now a professor in the Department of Theatre and Dance at the University of Hawai'i at Manoa. She has served as an associate editor for the *Journal of Asian Martial Arts*, and authored four articles dealing with Indonesian martial arts. Other works include *Theater & Martial Arts in West Sumatra: Randai & Silek of the Minangkabau* (Ohio University Press, 1999) and, on CD-ROM, *Randai: Folk Theater, Dance, and Martial Arts of West Sumatra* (University of Michigan Press, 2002). Dr. Pauka practices Japanese taiko drumming and trains in aikido, taekwondo, and silek. www.ohioswallow.com/author/Kirstin+Pauka

Mark V. Wiley, B.A., received his bachelor of arts degree in sociology from Drexel University. He began martial arts training in 1979 and has focused on Cabales Serrada Escrima under Grandmaster Angel Cabales. As an author, Wiley's works include *Filipino Martial Arts: Cabales Serrada Escrima* (Tuttle 1994) and *Filipino Fighting Arts: Theory and Practice* (Unique 2000). He has worked in the publishing field, including Tuttle Publishing and CFW Enterprises, and now is self-employed with Tambuli Media.

Silek:
The Martial Arts of the
Minangkabau in West Sumatra
by Kirstin Pauka, Ph.D.

All photographs courtesy of
Kirstin Pauka except where noted.

Background

"Silek" is the Minangkabau name for their indigenous version of martial arts known as silat in other parts of Indonesia and Malaysia.[1] For the Minangkabau, silek is an important element of their traditional culture. Within a matrilineal kinship system, all boys received silek training as soon as they were considered too old to live in their mother's house (around age twelve) and moved into the communal men's house (surau).[2] Silek was considered an integral part of boys' education once they had left childhood.[3] This is still very much the case at present although the matrilineal extended family structure is slowly being replaced by a patrilineal nuclear family due to the advance of Islam into West Sumatra. As a result, silek and Islam are interwoven and the Koran is often taught alongside silek in the communal men's house. Despite this, silek remains an important element of Minangkabau indigenous traditions and customs (adat) and is considered a valuable expression of their ethnic identity. Silek has been ever-present in everyday life, and consequently it is prominently featured in local folk tales, legends, proverbs, and other oral literature.

1

There is a large number of different indigenous types of silek throughout West Sumatra. Eleven major styles are recognized; these are Kumango, Lintau, Tuo, Sitaralak, Harimau, Pauh, Sungai Patai, Luncua, Gulo-Gulo Tareh, Baru, and Ulu Ambek.[4] These major styles are found in large areas of West Sumatra. Many more variations of silek are only found in restricted locations, often only in one village. In these cases, I will refer to them as "schools" rather than "styles." Many of these schools bear only the name of the village or region from which they originated and do not associate themselves with the major styles; some of them bear fancy names like *Harimau Lalok* ("Sleeping Tiger"), *Gajah Badorong* ("Charging Elephant"), *Kuciang Bagaluik* ("Playful Cat"), or *Puti Mandi* ("Bathing Princess"). All schools and styles trace their individual silek style back over many generations, its evolution interwoven with the Minangkabau origin myths or with Islam.[5]

Training Methods

The setting for silek training sessions is the *sasaran*, an open, empty space, preferably one close to the teacher's house. Training is almost exclusively held at night, after the Islamic evening prayers (*magrib*), and it lasts for two to three hours, sometimes until after midnight.[6] Most practice sessions are held in very dim light, often only relying on moonlight, a few torches, or a small gas lamp. This is not done for lack of stronger lights, but to train the eye as well as the intuition (or "inner power," *kebatinan*). Often there will be village elders around the training ground, casually chatting, singing, and playing instruments, mainly *talempong* (hand-held metal gongs) and *saluang* (bamboo flutes).[7]

Training typically includes none of the warm-ups known in other Asian martial arts. In silek, two partners of approximately the same physique and level of skill are paired and start "playing" (*main silek* is the standard term used for the training; *main* meaning "to play"). All this takes place under the close scrutiny of the teacher. Normally, only one pair plays at a time while the other students watch. Before starting, each pair goes through a standard opening ceremony which includes bows and stylized greetings, first towards the teacher and then towards each other. Then they start with the basic silek steps. Depending on the level of their skill, they will remain with the basics, often being interrupted and corrected by the teacher, or they will move on into a more advanced, free-style exchange of techniques. After several minutes, they stop and go through another greeting ceremony that consists of the same elements as the opening greeting, but in reversed order. Then a new pair comes up to the practice ground. The atmosphere during practice is normally relaxed; strenuous physical activity is not considered a high priority, nor is it indicative of effective training.

Two silek practitioners executing the formal greeting that precedes and ends each fighting sequence. They squat low to the ground, bring their hands to the ground and then lift them to their forehead. This movement is repeated in four directions. (Style: Sungai Patai)

Two silek opponents approach each other with *langkah*, or basic steps. Courtesy of Christine Martins. (Style: Silek Kumango)

The average time considered necessary to learn the basics of silek is between six and eight months. To develop a solid foundation, a student must train regularly for two to three years, and to become a *pandeka* (master), one has to train for at least fifteen years. Although silek was traditionally practiced by only males, today many *aliran* (martial arts schools) are open to females as well. A female student is always paired with another female, never with a male student, because physical contact between the sexes is considered improper; nonetheless, the male teacher often functions as a training partner for both sexes.

For training, most students wear either normal street clothing or the traditional silek outfit that consists of *galembong* (black long trousers), *taluak balango* (long-sleeved black shirt) and the *deta* (batik head wrap). A complete outfit also includes a *sampiang* (batik hip sash). Very often, the students only wear the galembong with a regular shirt or T-shirt during practice.[8] For more formal occasions (joint-training with other aliran, performances, or when visitors are present) the full costume is worn.

The learning process is based on observation and imitation, but the teacher often corrects the stance or execution of a movement by adjusting the student's limbs or posture. Rarely does a teacher explain a technique or an underlying concept to the student during practice.[9] However, after the training is over, most students linger around the teacher for quite some time, and he will often relate proverbs and tell stories, jokes or anecdotes related to silek.

Two female silek students practicing together.
(Style: Silek Kumango)

Students practice the same basic moves over and over again in several steps. First, they merely watch the senior students and the teacher. Then, they imitate the teacher, who executes the movements close to the students. Some aliran use a circular formation to simultaneously teach several students the basic steps. The teacher is part of the circle and the students glance at him from whatever angle is possible from their different positions, following his moves closely. Direct eye contact is not desired; instead, the students are encouraged to use their peripheral vision and intuition to pick up the teacher's movements. Often the teacher uses vocal cues or other sound cues, called *tapuak*, to indicate a change of direction or a new step. For this he claps his hands or slaps his leg with one hand.[10]

At a more advanced level, the student and his partner are on their own, with no visual guidance; they have to remember the techniques and rely on each other to complete the sequence. At this level, the teacher will often interrupt the sequence to give corrections. When he feels that both students have sufficiently grasped the technique and are able to remember it, he will move on to demonstrate a new sequence. Once students have learned the basics, they are encouraged to practice with other partners as well, thereby learning to adjust to a different anatomy, behavior and level of skill each time.

The formal outfit worn for silek: black, long-sleeved shirt, galembong pants with low crotch, sashes, and a head wrap.

An old silek master correcting his student's body position.
(Style: Silek Kumango).

Young boys practicing silek in a circular formation called galombang,
which is used to teach a group of beginners the basic steps.
This formation is also the origin of the circular martial arts
dances used in the Randai theatre of the region.

At this point, the students will be expected to "play continuously" (*main terus-menerus*). The basic strategic concept in this part of the training is *garak-garik*, best translated as "appropriate action and reaction." It can be explained by using the analogy of chess. As in chess, each new move has to be considered in relation to possible reactions. Each partner has several options at all times and attempts to choose the most effective one. One tries to anticipate the possible reactions of his partner and manipulate him into positions where he has fewer and fewer good options to choose. The game ends when one partner cannot respond with a technique anymore and is stuck in a lock or position with no way to get out of it; he then is declared "dead" (*mati*). The better and the more equally skilled the students are, the longer this kind of play can go on. Unlike in chess, the timing of each move is crucial. Each move has to be fast and precise and has to come as a surprise; otherwise the partner will anticipate and intercept the action before it can be executed.

Once the individual student has reached a high level of physical skill and is considered worthy of the teacher's trust, he will receive a specific and personal technique in a private meeting with his teacher. While bestowing this secret knowledge on his student, the teacher may recite mantras and prayers to insure that the technique will only be used in self-defense and will be successful.

Another level of training includes sending the student into the forest to meditate, conquer his fears, and survive for several days on his own. Another, less threatening, way of exposing students to outside forces is to let them participate in joint-training sessions and tournaments with other aliran. However, this is a recent development and during these meetings all participants are reminded not to reveal their best techniques because they might be learned by outsiders. Mutual friendly suspicion seems to prevail. On the highest level, a student can possibly learn fatal and magic techniques. The most feared are called *gayuang angin* ("hit by the wind")—magic, long-distance techniques that can be fatal, and *kebal*, a magic kind of inner strength that makes a person invulnerable.

Techniques & Strategies

The foundation of all silek moves are the steps called *langkah*. Each new student must master the basic steps before any other technique is taught. The first step instantly brings the practitioner from a neutral standing body position into the basic stance of silek. Placing the left foot forward and the right foot backward, he will glide into a low horse stance called *kudo-kudo*, the signature stance of silek. In this stance, the feet are about two shoulder widths apart, the left foot pointing forward, and the right turned to the outside at a 45°–90° angle, depending on the style. The knees are bent and the weight is mostly on the back foot. Some styles (e.g., Kumango) or schools (e.g., Harimau Sakti) emphasize an extremely low stance in which most of the weight is on the rear foot and the practitioner seems to be hovering just barely above the ground; other styles (e.g., Ulu Ambek) and schools (e.g., Bungo, Mangguang) prefer a higher stance with the weight more evenly distributed on both feet.

A silek master stepping into the basic
kudo-kudo stance. (Style: Silek Sitaralak)

7

In both versions, the torso is slightly bent forward at the waist, and the right arm extended forward in a soft inward curve at shoulder height; the left arm is held close to the body in a bent, guarding position. The head is straight, with the eyes not focused on any particular point, but rather taking the entire environment in through peripheral vision. This basic stance is used in the greeting and the stylized opening in which both partners step around each other and the training place before any advances or physical contacts between them occur. Depending on the style, this opening sequence can include three, four, nine or twelve such steps. Most schools classify themselves as belonging to either one of the *langkah tigo* (three steps), *langkah ampek* (four steps), *langkah sambilan* (nine steps), or *langkah duo-baleh* (twelve steps) styles. Some schools may use more than one langkah style depending on the context. The variations with just three of four steps are used for self-defense or in practice sessions in which both partners step around each other between attacks. The more elaborate step variations are often found in the opening of performances of silek and in fighting scenes within Randai theatre.

To move from one stance to another, the practitioner shifts his weight smoothly onto the front foot, while the back foot is lifted off the ground. Often practitioners will remain poised on one leg, before committing to one or another direction with the next step. This position is generally not considered a stance like the solid kudo-kudo, but a transition. It is a form of crane stance, either called *pitunggua*, if the lifted foot is slightly in front of the supporting leg, or *tagak itiak*, if the raised foot is tucked behind the bent knee of the supporting leg. In silek, especially in self-defense, both versions are very brief, whereas in performance contexts and in Randai they feature prominently and are held for longer periods of time to display the skill of the performers in keeping their balance. This is especially difficult on the uneven natural terrain on which silek is customarily done.

The second basic stance besides the kudo-kudo is called *gelek*. This stance is most easily reached directly from the kudo-kudo by merely twisting the upper body from one side to the other and by shifting the center of weight of the entire body towards the front while the feet stay in place. The main quality of the gelek is that it closes the body against a possible attack by means of the twist, and the front arm can easily execute a block or parry. In many styles this stance is even lower than the kudo-kudo.

A characteristic quality of all stepping techniques in silek is that they are executed very lightly and carefully, primarily to maintain agility and the ability to quickly position oneself for attack or defensive movements. Also, the practitioners are never permitted to look at the ground as this would distract them from the opponent. Therefore, they have to explore the terrain with their feet, scanning it for obstacles like roots, rocks, crevices, etc. This technique, called *pijak baro* (light step), is aptly described by a proverb of the Kumango style: "We have to see with our feet."

The silek practitioner on the right is retreating into a crane stance (*pitunggua*) as a defense against a leg sweep. (Style: Silek Kumango)

The silek practitioner on the right is using a dynamic crane stance (*tagak itiak*) as a transition into a retreating movement to evade the anticipated kick from his opponent. (Style: Silek Bungo)

A gelek turn with the left arm shielding the torso. (Style: Silek Bungo)

A very low gelek. (Style: Silek Kumango)

The next level of techniques involves *jurusan* (partner drills), standardized attack-defense sequences. They differ from school to school, but some shared foundations can be outlined here. For practice purposes, both partners assume different ready stances depending on who will execute the attack. The designated attacker will take a high stance with the left foot forward and the right hand in a cocked, preparatory position (*sikap pasang*) to indicate whether he will attack with a punch or variant strike.

Most schools use four basic initial attacks: a straight punch (*dorong*), a strike with the hand's edge aimed at the temple or neck coming in on a curve (*cokak rambah*), a strike to the top of the head coming down in a straight line (*cancang*), and a front kick aimed at the center of the body (*antam*). The defender will assume a different stance, either a kudo-kudo, exposing his center by opening both arms horizontally and offering the attacker his torso as a target, or he will stand in a totally upright neutral position. In either position, he has to be aware of the body parts that are most likely to be targeted for an attack. As soon as the attack is initiated, the defender has to decide on one of two main defensive options, whether he will move to the outside of the attacking limb or to the inside. In either case he will use the basic turning step gelek. This initial decisive move dictates what subsequent counter techniques he will be able to use. Beginners are generally first taught to move defensively to the outside, which is considered a safer position with regard to the attacker's other hand. After the first evasive move to either side of the attacker, the defender will attempt to apply a lock or hold on the attacker, rendering him immobile and thereby ending the attack. If the lock or hold is not effective, the attacker will continue to attack with different techniques until a final lock is reached.[11] The typical jurusan always ends with a defensive hold, pin, or lock, or with an evasive move, never with an attack technique.

Following three photographs:
A short partner drill (*jurusan*) that begins with the deflection of an attempted wrist grab and ends with a take-down through a head lock. (Notice the girls in the background, some of whom are the teacher's daughters and also participate in the practice). (School: Gadjah Badorong)

A practice session consists of several jurusan, typically starting with a simple type and progressing towards more complex and difficult variations. The basic pattern normally starts with a straight fist attack and consists of only two or three follow-up techniques, while the more advanced sequences are longer and include more difficult kicks and often ground techniques.

The ground techniques are considered the most difficult.[12] Moving on hands and feet, the practitioners have to assume the fluidity and quality of animal movements to move smoothly and effortlessly. Most styles (with the exception of Ulu Ambek) claim that the ground position is actually superior and gives the practitioner better control over the situation than a standing position.[13] This becomes clear when one sees how effortlessly these silek masters move low to the ground and how easily they can throw an opponent off balance through a leg sweep from underneath.

Following two photographs:
The student on the left attacks with *cancang* (straight strike to the top of the head).
The defender on the right moves to the outside of the arm and grabs the wrist
of his attacker. A wrist lock renders the practitioner on the right immobile.
(Style: Sungai Patai)

Following sequence representing Silek Sitaralak Style:
1) A student (left) thanks his master with a devotional
   bow for his guidance during practice.
2) The master (far right) with his students awaiting
   their turn during a competition. They all wear the
   complete formal silek costume, which is also used
   for the Randai theatre.
3-6) Master and student demonstrate various locks,
   holds, and pins.

Philosophical and Ethical Principles

Generally, each teacher has his own unique interpretation and philosophy about the appropriate ethics and aesthetics of silek. The most consistent and recurring aspects concern the defensive nature of this martial art and the ultimate achievements and qualities of a true master.

The most important aspect of silek, universally emphasized, is its defensive character. Silek may only be used to defend oneself or others in case of an attack, never to harm or coerce a non-aggressor, to gain power, or merely to impress others. This is expressed in one of the many proverbs about silek: "I do not seek trouble, but if I am met by an adversary, I shall not run away." The movement structure of silek is sometimes interpreted as reflecting this philosophy of non-aggression. The *langkah ampek* ("first four steps") have to be purely defensive movements consisting of blocks or parries.[14] Only if an aggressor attacks a fifth time is the defender allowed to use a counter-attack with a strike or kick. Should there be a sixth attack, he is allowed to use a more lethal technique to stun or potentially even to kill the attacker. The langkah ampek also has religious and philosophical significance. Generally the first four steps of any silek practice are intended to honor four entities in the following order: God, ancestors, parents, and teachers.[15]

Students are reminded that, before a physical confrontation ensues, they should attempt to deflect a potentially dangerous situation verbally. This is referred to as *silek lidah*, "martial arts of the tongue."

Silek may only be
used to defend
oneself or others in
case of an attack, never
to harm or coerce a
non-aggressor, to gain
power, or merely to
impress others.

Aesthetics

Besides its technical and ethical elements, silek has aesthetic standards. In silek, the beauty and function of movements are interrelated. Because silek is foremost an art of self-defense, only an effective technique is considered aesthetically pleasing. However, silek is also practiced and perceived as a performing art, and therefore secondary aesthetic values exist which relate not to its function but to its appearance. However, these primary and secondary values frequently overlap and both sets of aesthetic values are applied simultaneously. When asked how to define a well executed silek technique, most teachers list the following nine qualities: effectiveness, precision, control, speed, focus, balance, effortlessness, "lightfootedness," and fluidity. Generally, the first five are most important in relation to its function; the last four are more relevant to its outward appearance. All nine qualities are mandatory in either context; only the ranking of their importance is different. For example, effectiveness is most crucial in self-defense; without this quality silek could not serve its purpose, even if all the remaining eight qualities were present. To render a technique effective, obviously one has to execute it without losing one's balance or focus, so it is clear that all nine qualities are closely interrelated. All teachers claim that a well-executed technique looks beautiful and feels good; the aesthetic is both external and internal. Students develop the perception of what is aesthetically correct as well as effective as they observe their senior students and masters.

Magic

To various degrees, all silek styles include the use of magic, called *kebatinan*. Some of the magic practices also exist outside of and apart from silek, but here I will examine only those that are found in the context of silek. Magic is not generally displayed publicly, and access to information about magical practices is very limited. In one prominent silek style, Ulu Ambek, the practitioners fight almost without physical contact. Although they come close to each other in combat, an attack always stops several inches before actually touching. This phenomenon is explained as magic coming from an inner power source (*tenaga batin*), which is achieved through years of meditation, exercise, fasting, and strong faith. This inner strength enables the defender to stop any attack before it can reach his body and do harm. The use of magic is purely defensive and it may be best described as an invisible shield that the defender creates around his body. Often a master can extend his protective shield to include his students or close relatives and protect them against physical harm or black magic intended to manipulate the victim's behavior. During competitions between silek groups, the younger performers tend to be protected through the magic shield of their teachers, who sit at the edges of the compound and chant mantras, thereby transferring some of their magic power to the students.[16]

The knowledge and application of magic (*ilmu batin*) is divided into evil (black) and good (white) magic. The protective shield used by Ulu Ambek practitioners is classified as white magic (*ilmu putih*), and so are most other magic practices that are used within the context of silek. Besides the inner power that can be developed by gifted individuals through meditation, fasting, and exercise, there is also a vast outside power field that some individuals can access. According to pre-Islamic beliefs, this outside field is inhabited by positive and negative spirits which can be called upon for help, but this contact with the spirit world is considered dangerous and can only be established by the most proficient masters.

Several silek masters I met were also *dukun* (traditional shamans, healers and masters of *ilmu putih*). Some of their magic abilities included the summoning of spirits of deceased persons who would enter their bodies and speak with their voices. In one case, a dukun claimed to be able to summon the spirit of an ancestor, also a silek master. This spirit could, upon request, enable him to perform extraordinary silek techniques.[17] Other magical activities include the fabrication of amulets (*jimat*) which, along with mantras, teachers give to their students for protection. On another occasion, I witnessed the performance of *dabuih*, the Minangkabau version of a kind of self-mutilation (called *dabus* in other regions of Indonesia), in which the performer uses a sharp sword to pierce and slash himself and his students, but without inflicting injuries. The performer was a member of the *tarikat*, a mystical organization of Islamic scholars. He claimed that his magical ability was based on his strong faith in Allah. In this incident, as in many others, pre-Islamic practices and orthodox Islamic beliefs are intertwined.

Theatrical Aspects of Silek

Several inherent characteristics of silek give its execution dance-like qualities. As we saw above, silek is often accompanied by music and song during which the musicians match the movements of the combatants and highlight dramatic moments in the combat with their music. Another unique feature is the circular training form (*galombang*) that is used by some aliran. In this practice, all participants execute the same movements simultaneously, giving it a dance-like character. Having inherent features with an affinity to dance and theatre, it is not surprising that silek constitutes the origin of most Minangkabau dance forms and of other performance arts, most prominently the Randai folk theatre.[18]

A striking example of how silek is used in a dramatic dance is the *tari tanduak* (horn dance).[19] This mini-dance or drama features an ensemble of three silek performers, four musicians, and one banner carrier. The most outstanding features, however, are the hand-held props that are used: two huge kites and an umbrella. The performers move exclusively with silek steps, enacting a legendary combat from Minangkabau history.

Tari Rantak, a dance that has developed out of silek, is also performed by women.

A musician accompanies a silek performance on the seated talempong.

The plot of the drama is simple and involves two feuding kingdoms (Jambulipo and Sosai Gunuang Medan). Each kingdom is represented by four lineage heads (datuak), which, in turn, are symbolized by the four horns (tanduak) on each of the kites. The legendary conflict erupted over land claims. The battle continued undecided until finally the king of the Minangkabau intervened by sending his royal umbrella to the battlefield, thereby signaling that he desired an end to the conflict.[20]

18

The reenactment of this battle story starts with a slow-paced musical piece played on two oblong drums (*gendang sarunai*) and two hand-held metal gongs (*talempong*). The two kites are propped up and displayed in the center of the performance space. Then two silek performers enter the performance space with the customary opening steps and greetings. They then grab their kites while the musicians pick up the pace. The ensuing fight is executed with increasing speed and excitement, during which the performers move exclusively with silek steps and thrust the kites toward each other. After each encounter, they retreat to the edge of the performance space, the music gets faster, and they prepare for a new attack. At the climax of the combat, the banner at the edge of the circle is waved and a third silek performer moves into the circle carrying the umbrella. He moves with much slower silek steps than the two fighting opponents, but he manages nonetheless to drive them apart and appease them. They stop fighting and the props are planted in the center. The music slows to a medium pace while the performers execute the closing steps and traditional greeting as in the beginning of the performance.

The musical ensemble that accompanies the tari tanduak consists of two gendang drums and two hand-held talempong gongs. These two drums have been passed down for fourteen generations and are said to house spirits.

Close-up of a horned kite. It is decorated with
mirrors and emblems signifying the warring
factions. At the climax of the tari tanduak, the
third silek master enters the performance space
carrying the royal umbrella to end the battle.

This silek performance constitutes a dance-drama in embryonic form and
represents an early stage in the development of a full-fledged drama. The most
remarkable characteristic is the continuous presence of silek movements
throughout the entire performance. Many other performance events can be found
on the continuum between silek and theatre. They have had considerable influence on silek itself in the past. In public demonstrations of "pure" silek, dance
and theatrical elements from other performance arts resurface and make for a
dynamic exchange among these Minangkabau art forms, enriching their repertoire
in the process.

Notes

1 This article is based on my research in West Sumatra in 1994. I studied silek for nine months with teachers of the following different styles or schools: Silek Kumango, Silek Harimau, Gadjah Badorong and Puti Mandi. These four were chosen to cover two of the major styles and two smaller schools. I also surveyed other styles in relation to the dance and theatre arts of the region (Pauka, 1995a).

2 Traditionally, families live in the mother's Big House (*rumah gadang*), but only daughters stay with their mothers after puberty. Boys and unmarried young men sleep in the *surau*, a communal men's house. After marriage, they sleep in their wives' rooms, in their mother-in-laws' homes. This is part of the matrilocal and matrilineal social structure of the Minangkabau, which prescribes that the mother owns house and property and passes it on to her daughters (despite the fact that today the Minangkabau are Moslems). However, today the *rumah gadang* and its life style are slowly being replaced by smaller patrilineal families in the larger villages and cities. In the highlands of West Sumatra the traditional life style is still intact.

3 Nowadays, girls are also allowed to participate in traditional silek practice, but few do so (about one out of ten silek students is female). Most often it is the daughters of silek teachers who are present during practice and who eventually participate actively or participate in silek as it is taught in the public schools as part of physical education.

4 This classification is based on the wide distribution of these styles. Hiltrud Cordes (1990: 92–95) lists only the first ten as major styles; however, according to my research, we should add Ulu Ambek to this list. It is a style dominant in the entire coastal Pariaman area and well-known throughout the entire Minangkabau region (Pauka, 1996).

5 The origins of West Sumatran silek cannot be traced sufficiently, due to the lack of written documentation, but one of the most compelling origin theories is that Indian martial arts found their way to Sumatra around the eighth century during the Srivijaya kingdom (Draeger, 1972; Alexander, 1970). The Minangkabau themselves have their own origin myths of silek that often differ greatly from the theories of Western researchers. Minangkabau origin myths are abundant and colorful, as is often the case in oral traditions. Generally speaking, there are three types of origin myths for silek.

    Some styles or schools trace their specific origin back to an historical person or persons, typically three to ten generations ago, who then passed their skills on to sons and grandsons. This type of origin story often includes information that the original teacher received his skill through some magic power, acquired either while sleeping, after having fainted, or perhaps during a thunderstorm or some other natural disturbance. Other schools, citing the epic origin myth of the Minangkabau people, credit the two legendary ancestors with the invention and development of silek.

A third frequently heard origin myth is Islam-based. Some silek teachers credit Adam, or Cain and Abel, or even the Archangel Gabriel with the invention of silek. Then, the story goes, they passed it on in some mysterious way to one of the ancestors of a specific aliran. Often they employed the same "tool" of sleep-teaching, fainting spells, and other magical devices. One can see how these transmission "tools" can easily be linked to the more indigenous origin myths mentioned above in an attempt to connect Minangkabau history and Islam. This religious origin myth highlights the strong desire of the teachers to synthesize and to weave an historical tapestry that connects religion and Minangkabau history and legends about martial arts. This synthesis can also be seen in the fact that after the arrival of Islam the communal surau was converted into a part of the mosque that now serves a multitude of community functions, including Koran lessons, silek training, and practice for the local folk theatre form called "Randai."

6 Midnight is considered an auspicious time, when magic powers are penetrating the human sphere. It can, at the same time, be dangerous and rewarding to practice at that time. Many stories relate that a master acquired some magical skill at midnight, but I have not seen any special event at midnight although I have been present during many midnight practice sessions. For the younger children, the training ends around ten o'clock for two reasons; one is the fear that they might be exposed to dangerous magical powers at midnight and the other is the more practical consideration that they get enough sleep before attending school the next morning.

7 The presence of musicians becomes more formalized when guests (for example, practitioners from a neighboring sasaran) are present. Then the musicians will wear traditional costume, be seated on a special mat, and play throughout the entire event. For regular training sessions, their presence is not mandatory, but welcomed.

8 I was repeatedly informed that many students are too poor to buy the silek outfit, which costs around 8,000 rupiah, about 4 US dollars. (The daily pay of an unskilled worker is about 5,000 rupiah.)

9 This was different in my case; many teachers went out of their way to explain techniques. When asked for names or concepts of specific movements, they often used proverbs or metaphors like animal behavior and images from nature to explain a technique.

10 This circular formation in silek practice as well as the sound cues are also main features of the theatre-form Randai which was derived from silek.

11 Often the defender will allow the attacker to escape the defensive lock or hold in order to continue the sequence and practice more variations within a single jurusan.

12 Even more difficult are techniques used in combination with magic.

13 Ulu Ambek relies more on magic and does not emphasize low stances or ground techniques.

14 Personal interview with Pak Azur, teacher of Silek Kumango (Sianau Indah, Tanah Datar, June 1994).

15 The number four is used symbolically in the context of many Asian philosophies (Bertling, 1954). In relation to silek, it is also often used to refer to four general conditions to be relied on in silek and in life in general. These are given to man through birth by four entities: mother, father, nature, and God (personal interview with Pak Agung, teacher of Silek Gajah Badorong, Baruh Bukit, July 1994). The one given by the mother is further divided into four sub-units: skin, blood, flesh, and bone. Liver, heart, spleen, and kidneys are obtained from the father. Nature supplied man with fire, water, air, and land. God gives the soul. The number four is probably the most significant and important one in silek and in the Minangkabau culture generally. Most silek techniques are divided into groups of four: four major attacks, four major defenses, etc.

16 It is said that this protective shield can also preempt an attack altogether. The best silek master is the one that does not get into fights at all because his potential attackers sense his strength and promptly flee.

17 I have never witnessed a spirit descend into a medium or shaman. The account was described to me in much detail, however, and by two independent sources. The summoning of a spirit was once attempted in my presence, but was unsuccessful. It was explained to me that the spirits are capricious and will not come when a stranger is present, no matter how benevolent one's intention or how unobtrusive one's behavior.

18 The main dance forms are *tari ratak* (fighting dance), *tari piriang* (plate dance), *tari tanduak* (horn dance), and *tari pasambahan* (welcoming dance).

19 The tari tanduak is performed in the Lubuk Tarab district of the Sijunjung province in West Sumatra.

20 From the middle of the fourteenth to the middle of the nineteenth century, West Sumatra was ruled by a royal family. Besides paying tribute, however, the various provinces largely retained their autonomy so that the king had no power to meddle with their internal affairs (de Jong, 1980: 8). His only means of interference was the said royal umbrella, which had symbolic powers only.

Bibliography

Alexander, H., et al. (1970). *Pentjak silat: The Indonesian fighting art.* Rutland, VT: Charles E. Tuttle.

Bertling, C. (1954). Vierzahl, kreuz und mandala in Asien. *Bijdragen tot de Taal-Land-en Volkenkunde van Nederlandsch-Indië,* 110, 93–115.

Cordes, H. (1990). Pencak silat: Die kampfkunst der Minangkabau und ihr ku turelles umfeld. Ph.D. dissertation, University of Köln.

de Jong, P. (1980). *Minangkabau and Negri sembilan–Socio-political structure in Indonesia.* The Hage: Martinus Nijhoff.

Draeger, D. (1969). *Comprehensive Asian fighting arts.* Rutland, VT: Charles E. Tuttle.

Draeger, D. (1972). *Weapons and fighting arts of the Indonesian archipelago.* Rutland, VT: Charles E. Tuttle.

Pauka, K. (1995). Martial arts, magic, and male bonding: The pauleh tinggi ceremony of West Sumatra. *Journal of Asian Martial Arts,* 4(3), 26–45.

Pauka, K. (1996). Conflict and combat in performance: An analysis of the Randai folk theatre of the Minangkabau in West Sumatra. Ph.D. dissertation with CD-ROM, University of Hawaii.

A Flower of Martial Arts:
The Randai Folk Theatre of
the Minangkabau in West Sumatra
by Kirstin Pauka, Ph.D.

Randai theatre includes a large repertoire of martial arts techniques.
Two rows of Randai performers enter the performance
space and pose in a greeting position.
Photography by K. Pauka except where noted.

Introduction*

A Randai event is typically preceded by an exciting tapestry of sound that announces to the villagers that the theatre troupe has arrived and a performance is about to begin. As soon as the audience has assembled around the empty open-air lot, an even number of dancers enters the performance space in two lines. Accompanied by a musical introduction, the dancers move into the center with martial arts steps and then pose in a humble greeting position low to the ground (see photo). In this pose they sing a welcome to the audience, asking forgiveness in case they should make any mistakes and requesting benevolent attention.

Another short martial arts dance in which the two lines of dancers converge in a circular formation follows the welcoming. Then the dancers sit down. One or two of them step into the center of the circle to reiterate the greeting and announce the story to be performed.

* This article is a revised version of an article that was previously published in the *Asian Theatre Journal* (Fall 1996) under the same title.

Most Randai stories are based on old Minangkabau legends detailing the struggles and adventures of local folk heroes. These tales often feature conflicts of interest within the complex clan structure of Minangkabau society. They also contain romance, intrigue, and combat. After the story is announced, another dance follows, accompanied by an introductory song that sets the mood for the first scene to be enacted. Then two or more members step inside the circle to deliver the speeches of the first scene. The remaining members of the circle sit and watch quietly until, after the last words are spoken, they rise at once at the vocal cue of the circle leader and perform a different martial arts dance to a new song. This mixture of enacted scenes and martial dances continues for several hours and typically culminates in a major fighting scene which resolves the central conflict (photo below). A final dance is then performed to a standard closing song, indicating the end of the performance. The performers file out of the circle in two lines and the spectators disperse to the nearby food booths or to a neighbor's house to discuss the performance.

Martial arts constitute the core of the movement repertoire of the Randai folk theatre. According to an old Minangkabau proverb, Randai is a "flower of silek." *Silek* is the name for the indigenous martial arts form of the Minangkabau ethnic group in West Sumatra, Indonesia. Randai today is a composite art form combining martial arts, music, dance, and acting. It can be considered a "flowering" of silek in two major ways: in terms of its origin and in terms of its performance features.

A Randai fighting scene. The attacker is lunging with a sharp-bladed knife which is successfully blocked with a counter technique.

Three Randai actors deliver their lines inside the circle.
The dancers crouch quietly and wait for their cue to get up
and perform the galombang dance between scenes.

Origin

Randai theatre is said to have evolved out of the martial arts, specifically out of a circular martial dance called *dampeang*.[1] Although there is some controversy over the details of this evolutionary process and other origin theories do exist, the following theory is the most significant and plausible.[2]

To practice basic silek moves, many *aliran silek* (martial art schools) employ one-on-one exercises and also a circular constellation with an even number of participants. In this circular formation, the students observe the leader and imitate his moves as closely as possible to learn the basics. Silek is traditionally accompanied by music which helps the students to move rhythmically and closely follow the teacher's movements. Once the students become proficient in the basic form, they advance to a more mystical level known as *dampeang* or *dampeng*, a circular martial dance which promotes the enhancement of their sixth sense and premonition. This circular dance serves as the foundation for the aestheticized martial movements employed in the *galombang* dance in Randai:

> Dampeng dancers entered into a state of trance during which they were able to perform abnormal physical feats which made the display more exciting and impressive. Especially in pre-Muslim times (and also to adegree since Islam became the dominant religion), it was believed that dancers in a state of trance were able to contact the spirits, especially the spirits of the ancestors, for the sake of obtaining clairvoyance and spirit blessings for the common good and to avert calamities from happening.   —Kartomi, 1981:15

Dampeang dance with this mystical quality can still be found in the coastal Pariaman area, but it is almost extinct in other parts of West Sumatra.[3] Simple circular practices devoid of the mystical aspect are fairly common.

The lyrics employed in the dampeang became more elaborate over the years and incorporated preexisting Minangkabau stories (*kaba*) that told of ancestors, warriors, and heroes. With this inclusion of kaba, one further significant step was taken toward a more complex form of Randai. Another crucial addition came when some members reputedly stepped inside the circle to enact a fighting scene that was described in the song's lyrics.[4] During this enactment, the other members stopped their silek dance and sat down to watch. This formation is now the basic spatial composition of Randai acting scenes. After the fighting scene, they resumed the circular martial arts dance.

Over the years other scenes besides fighting scenes were also acted out. Interestingly, the actors used silek moves in these new nonfighting scenes as well. In the beginning of this new development the story was still told by the singers, but the actors quickly took over and transformed the narratives into simple dialogue sections. At that time the silek participants were still all male. When the stories became progressively more complex, female roles became necessary and were enacted by males. Chosen for their beauty and grace, these actors became known as *bujang gadih* ("boy-girls"). This unique tradition can still be seen today, although the number of all-male groups is declining rapidly.[5]

FIGURE 1: Female performers in active Randai groups in 1994.
Only 2% of all groups surveyed are all-male. The majority have had female performers since the founding of the group. These were mainly groups that were founded after 1975. This and the following graphs are based on questionnnaire answers that were provided by 102 Randai groups participating in the Fifth West Sumatra Randai Festival in 1994. For more statistical data on the present state of Randai groups see Pauka (1996: 223–239).

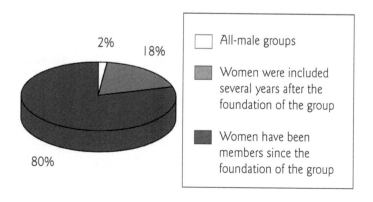

This origin theory, then, gives a believable account of the "flowering" of silek and the emergence of Randai.[6] By the turn of the century Randai in its basic form consisted of circular martial dances, poetic storytelling, and songs. Possibly a simple form of acting and dialogue was already part of it. At the beginning of the twentieth century, the Malay *bangsawan* comedy appeared in the West Sumatra region where it was introduced via traveling troupes (Harun, 1992: 77). Quickly becoming a popular folk entertainment, it is believed to have influenced the further development of Randai, mainly its acting style.[7]

A major change came in the mid-1960s, when female performers started to act the female roles. This was the result of at least three separate developments. First, female performers had long been popular as folk singers in the art form known as *saluang jo dendang* (flute and song), which was adopted into Randai. Second, this development was, if not openly welcomed, at least quickly accepted by the Islamic religious leaders who had been opposed to the female impersonator (*bujang gadih*) all along, condemning it as a perversion. Third, the new Indonesian government established academies for the performing arts which started to teach regional folk arts including Randai.[8] As these schools were open to both male and female students, for the first time females were allowed to learn and practice all aspects of Randai. Today women constitute about one-fourth of the members of each of the over two hundred active troupes.

Silek's Influence

Silek's strong influence on Randai manifests itself on two levels: it is featured thematically in the stories, and it constitutes the foundation of the movement repertoire. The Randai story material incorporates silek in several principal ways. As most of the characters, male and female, are proficient in silek, it is ever-present in most of the stories. The quest for good silek training by many male characters in connection with their journeying illustrates that silek is seen as an indispensable part of the education of young men. Silek masters are generally portrayed as wise, kind, and virtuous; students seeking knowledge and silek mastery are depicted as maturing, positive role models in the plays.

Besides being featured as an important skill of every main character, silek is also central to the development of the plot and is often employed in the resolution of conflicts. Typically conflicts arise, escalate, and then culminate in a silek confrontation. Basic philosophical concepts of silek are also integral to the plays. A virtuous hero, for instance, is portrayed as obeying the central ethical rule of silek: to use it solely as a means of self-defense. Since fighting in Randai plays tends to be resolved in a way that propagates proper behavior, conflict scenarios, fighting scenes and conflict resolution serve as vehicles of moral instruction. Good characters typically prevail; evil ones either perish or are redeemed.

The movement repertoire in Randai is clearly a "flower of silek." To perform in Randai, basic martial arts skills are mandatory; consequently, most performers are proficient in silek. Two steps in the development of Randai can still be seen as part of its current performance features: the fighting scenes and the galombang circular martial dance. Movements in the fighting scenes are simply called *main silek* (play silek), indicating that they are perceived as "pure" silek moves, since the term main silek is also used for regular silek practice. Silek movements in the galombang, however, have undergone significant changes and become more dance-like.

Fighting Scenes

Fighting scenes are of great variety—ranging from short encounters of only three or four exchanges of attack and defense to long scenes with multiple encounters between several characters. These scenes can consist of pure silek sequences or of silek interspersed with theatrical elements like acrobatics, clowning, and physical and verbal jokes. Weapons are a vital part of combat and figure prominently in Randai.

A Randai fighting scene. The actor on the left is about to apply an elbow strike to the throat of his opponent. The leader of the galombang observes the scene, waiting for the last words after which he will give a loud vocal cue to the other galombang dancers to start.

A frequent, almost stereotypical, fighting scene involves the protagonist and a gang of three or four villains. Typically they will engage in a heated verbal encounter (called *silek lida*, "martial arts of the tongue") before the actual physical attacks begin. One of the robbers attacks first—often shoved into that role by his partners in crime who are too cowardly to attack the hero themselves. After defending himself against each of the attackers individually, the protagonist is then faced with a new level of attack in which the robbers team up and attack as a group. The scene therefore features one-on-one fighting sequences as well as sequences with multiple attackers, a constellation that is also practiced by advanced students in silek training sessions. Frequently, all the attackers are subdued and pinned to the ground with a pin called *kunci mati* (death lock). This technique is applied to their wrists or ankles in such a way that escape is impossible. On rare occasions the hero is overwhelmed and taken prisoner by the robbers.

Left: An actor in a low silek stance prior to engaging in combat with his opponent. Photograph courtesy of Edy Utama. Right: The *guru-tuo silek* (martial arts master) of a Randai group intently observes the performance of his students from the edge of the performance space.

The robber scene is the most frequently played scene in Randai for four reasons. First, since most of the plays contain a travel scene, it can be built into almost any play. Outdoors, attackers can find an easy target in someone who is on the road alone. Second, the robber scene is highly popular with the audience because it mixes serious fighting with clowning and joking. Third, it has didactic implications, instructing the audience that living as a robber is immoral and will normally end in defeat and disgrace. Fourth, it incorporates long sequences with multiple attackers and thereby allows for the display of a large repertoire of silek techniques. Robber scenes are integral to the story line. In many stories a female character is attacked by robbers while on the road and a stranger comes to her rescue. Predictably the woman then falls in love with the stranger and desires to marry him. This, in turn, often creates the story's main conflict, especially if her family has already chosen a husband for her.

The following example from the performance of the play *Maelo Rambuik Dalam Tapuang* ("Pulling Hair from the Flour") describes a standard Randai plot with a silek fighting scene at the climax of the play. The story leading up to the fight is fairly simple and can be briefly recounted here. The young maiden Bainai is ordered by her father to marry Sutan Lembang Alam (Prince of Nature), an arrangement that was agreed to by both families years ago. But Lembang is an immature hothead, prone to gambling, and without manners. Bainai dislikes him for good reason. Besides, she already has a sweetheart, Sutan Nagari (Prince of the District), but when she resists the match, her father curses and abandons her. She is ready to kill herself when her uncle takes pity on her and helps arrange a wedding between the two young lovers. The disgruntled ex-fiance, publicly disgraced and ridiculed, is enraged and driven only by thoughts of revenge. He confronts Bainai and Nagari with the intention of murdering them both. The physical fighting scene is preceded by a verbal challenge uttered by Lembang in which he brags about his fighting skills. Nagari attempts to calm him and bring him to reason to no avail, and the battle begins. Three other characters are present during this scene: Bainai, who basically stays at the fringe of the action, and two friends of Lembang. Although these two friends initially enjoy the intensifying confrontation and make comments and jokes on the side, when the fight turns serious they try to interrupt it. Nagari wins the fight, but he spares the life of his adversary. Bainai's uncle rushes to the scene and lectures the young people about proper behavior. The offender apologizes and is sent to the *rantau*.

The physical fighting is accompanied by a lively tune played by the talempong orchestra which starts quietly during the verbal confrontation and becomes increasingly louder as the fighting scene intensifies. The opponents take their positions on opposite sides of the circle, both posing in a low stance called *kudo-kudo* (horse stance). From there they move in unison through a short opening sequence consisting of slow steps, fast body turns, and poses in very low stances (see previous photo). This is identical to the traditional preliminary sequence that precedes every practice encounter in silek. Its purpose is to show respect to the teachers, elders, and training partners, and to help the practitioner focus and find his balance. In Randai this opening sequence serves similar purposes: to show respect and enhance focus. In addition, it is a highly theatrical device to attract the spectators' attention. After the opening, a total of four standard attack and defense sequences (called *jurusan*) are performed: the first three empty-handed, the last one with a dagger. Between the four individual sequences, the opponents retreat to their positions on the perimeter of the circle and repeat the movement sequence from the beginning in abbreviated form as an interlude between attacks.

In Randai combat there is generally a progression of difficulty and excitement in the sense that the techniques used in the first jurusan are simpler than the following ones. The fighting typically moves from standing techniques to ground techniques and then to weapons. Each jurusan has a specific focus. In the play described here, the first jurusan consists mainly of kicking techniques. The second focuses on hand techniques and includes a grappling technique and a recovery in the form of a front roll. The third jurusan starts with kicking techniques followed by a take-down and subsequent ground kicking techniques and some acrobatics. The fourth and last sequence features dangerous knife combat with a sharp weapon. This progression reflects the various levels of silek training from the simple standing techniques to the more complicated ground fighting and dangerous weapon techniques. The only exception to this progression is an advanced defense move at the beginning of the first jurusan. Called *sapik kalo* (scorpion strike), this strike to the throat is extremely difficult to execute properly and therefore quite dangerous. This advanced technique is used dramatically in the beginning of the combat to capture the audience's attention and display virtuosity as a stunning opening.

Two opponents circle each other in an opening sequence of a fighting scene.

FIGURE 2: Silek Proficiency of Randai Performers

Seventy-six percent of all groups surveyed state that all their performers are proficient in silek. Seventeen percent of the groups state that almost all members are proficient; this typically means that all the galombang members are proficient, but some actors or musicians might not be. A few groups (less than 10%) have a proficiency rate of half or less than half of the members.

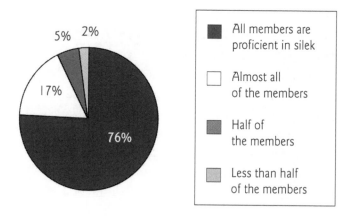

The progression in difficulty is also used dramatically to build tension and excitement. This fighting scene illustrates how actual silek jurusan are used in the theatrical context. Like the opening sequence, all four jurusan are basically authentic practice jurusan selected from the local silek style of the Padang Pariaman region (silek pauh). However, they are modified slightly for added theatrical effect. For example, they include kicks to the head level (instead of the customary torso level), which is perceived as more exciting and difficult. An acrobatic finish (forward flips) in the third jurusan is not part of the traditional form either, but is added for theatrical effect. Moreover, the execution of the techniques is typically faster in Randai than in a silek practice session. In silek training, the practitioner's intent is to learn the moves and improve the details. Therefore a movement sequence will often be repeated slowly, several times, until both partners can execute it rapidly and precisely. In performance, however, the preset sequences are highly rehearsed and faster, which is also more exciting for the audience. According to the performers, fighting scenes have to look "real" if they are to be well received by the spectators. Consequently the movements have to be executed with considerable speed, and the attacks and defenses have to come as close as possible to the target without actually inflicting injury.

In sum, then, although Randai fighting scenes are based on authentic silek techniques, they undergo transformations in the theatrical context and truly become "flowers of silek."

Left: Two fighters are engaged in ground combat. The one on the left recovers from a take-down by maneuvering into a flip. Right: Galombang dancers execute a jurusan, a set attack-defense sequence, that ends with an elbow-lock.

Galombang dancers surround the singers and flute player.

The Circular Martial Arts Dance

Between scenes, the circular martial arts dance known as *galombang* is performed by ten to eighteen dancers, while two singers and a flute player stand in the center of the circle and present a song as a transition from one scene to the next. Typically the singers recapitulate what happened in the previous scene and introduce what is about to follow, thereby establishing the mood, time, and location for the next scene. Silek movements from fighting scenes reappear regularly in this galombang dance in the form of basic steps and short jurusan.

Each galombang dance consists of several parts: an opening bridge, several basic silek moves and one jurusan performed during each song verse, percussive sequences between verses, and a closing bridge.

Galombang dancers execute a *jurusan*, a set attack-defense sequence, choreographed here with a kicking attack and an ankle-lock as defense. Photograph courtesy of Edy Utama.

The opening bridge begins immediately after a scene is finished, while the actors remain standing in the center of the circle. The galombang members get up from their seated position and move with silek steps toward the actors in the center. Upon meeting, the male characters from the scene become galombang members and execute the same movements when the circle moves outward again. The male characters seemingly "disappear" into the galombang. At the same time, female characters leave the circle and change places with the singers, who then move to the center of the circle and start the song. The opening bridge therefore facilitates a smooth transition between the end of a scene and the beginning of a song and is aptly called *garak panghubung ka gurindam* (movement connecting to the song). The closing bridge does the same in reverse and is called *garak panghubung ka curito* (movement connecting to the story). Both bridges consist strictly of silek moves and percussive patterns called *tapuak*.

Each song consists of several verses during which the dancers perform a series of silek moves. As these often include short jurusan which are executed in pairs, an even number of circle members is mandatory. The same movement sequence is repeated for each new verse of the song and also ended by the same percussive tapuak pattern. After the tapuak, the performers often walk a few steps until the singer begins the next verse. As soon as the singers have finished the song, the dancers conclude the galombang by a closing bridge that has a similar function to that of the opening bridge. It allows a smooth transition and exchange of singers and actors in the center of the circle. Again, some of the galombang members "reappear" as characters in the scene.

For each new song a new galombang with different subunits is performed. The jurusan are usually built into the main body of the galombang. Although some groups prefer to integrate them into the opening or closing bridge, these are exceptions. Most groups favor the display of their jurusan several times within one galombang, once in each verse, rather than only once within one single opening or closing bridge, possibly because these sequences are generally considered highlights within the galombang. When executed quickly and precisely, the jurusan never fails to delight the spectators, who evaluate the performers' silek skills by how well they execute these drills. Most groups include them in at least half of their galombang circles.

Female galombang dancers perform in unison.

Jurusan in the circular dance are typically shorter than the ones used in fighting scenes and consist of only two to four attacks and defenses. Since these moves are performed in time to the song melody and must be executed simultaneously by all members of the circle, they are also generally done at a somewhat more even pace than in a combat scene. The performers strive to move in unison by following the movements and vocal cues of the pambalok galombang (circle leader) closely. Therefore they have to focus on the leader and, at the same time, on their partner so they do not accidentally hit or kick him or her. They execute

37

their movements in the same constellation in each verse and repeat them as often as the singer sings a new song. At all times their direction of movement is in relation to the circular formation and in relation to the other circle members. The combination of all these elements—the even pace, the synchronicity, the circular orientation, the focus on the leader, the repetitiveness—gives the silek moves in the galombang a more dance-like quality than the execution of "pure" silek moves practiced by combatants in a fighting scene. This dance-like quality is another reason why Randai is called a "flower of silek."

Percussive sequences performed by the dancers add to this dance-like quality and, as noted, are referred to as tapuak. Also derived from silek techniques, they can be considered another "blossom" of the martial arts. These tapuak are typically performed between the verses of each song. Two types of tapuak exist: *tapuak galembong* (slapping the pants) and *tapuak tangan* (clapping the hands). The tapuak galembong can be considered the signature technique of Randai; when performed correctly and by all performers simultaneously, it produces the magnificent drum-like sounds that are responsible for much of the excitement Randai creates.

The tapuak galembong is a technique derived from two kinds of slapping techniques used in silek. In the first variation, the practitioner slaps his thigh, hip, or torso with one hand while stepping forward or backward. This is intended as a signal that alerts the partner in practice or distracts an opponent in a tournament. A second variation within silek is a high frontal kick which stretches the wide fabric of the pants. The fabric is hit with both hands simultaneously while the kick is executed, when the leg is in its highest position. This variation can most frequently be observed when silek is performed as entertainment, or demonstration, and is intended to draw the audience's attention to the attack.

From these simple slapping techniques used in silek, Randai performers have developed an impressive percussive repertoire. In addition to the simple frontal kick with the slap, similar slaps are now executed while the leg is raised to one side, in the process of stepping forward or backward, and even while turning and spinning. With each step the leg swings up high toward a ninety-degree angle. Since the creation of a strong slapping sound is crucial, the leg must swing out and up in time to reach the highest point at the precise moment the slap has to be performed. To produce the desired sound, the hands come in toward the fabric from the outside and the inside of the leg. At the instant of the hit, the hands do not actually contact each other, as in a hand clap, but pass each other closely, thereby stretching the fabric to produce the sound. It is the fabric being hit and stretched that creates the sound, not the hands actually touching each other through the fabric.

Tapuak galembang (pants slapping) while stepping forward.

Another main tapuak technique consists of the following constellation. Both feet are on the ground. The torso is bent slightly forward and both hands hit the front of the stretched fabric between the legs. At the instant of impact, the knees are jerked apart slightly to give the fabric the extra bounce to produce a loud and sharp sound. Experts can time this so well that the sound actually changes from low to high as the fabric is stretched. Sounds can also be altered by spreading or closing the fingers and by modifying the intensity with which the blows are struck.

Patterns of individual slaps and claps are composed into simple or complex sequences, depending on the skills of the performers and the preferences of the galombang leader. Scores and scores of different rhythms exist. Within a single song, the percussive sequences between verses are generally the same and are cued and led by the leader of the circle through vocal sounds like "hep" and "ta." These vocal cues are an integral part of the percussive pattern and also serve to coordinate and synchronize the movements and sounds of the performers.

Besides the standard sounds of hand clapping and slaps on stretched fabric, there are several other percussive sounds like finger snapping and the slapping of body parts such as thighs, chests or forearms. Some of these again stem from silek techniques and have been transformed into a musical and theatrical element in Randai. Choral tapuak patterns are often performed by splitting the circle members into two groups. Groups A and B play different patterns that are intricately interlocked. A standard formation for this choral tapuak is illustrated in Figure 3. An interesting variation of this arrangement is performed when only the two galombang leaders play pattern A and the rest of the group play pattern B. In this variation, the two leaders leave the circular formation and enter the center of the circle for the tapuak sequence. Thus the sound differentiation is made visible by the spatial separation of the two groups. In this variation, the singers and flute player stay outside the circle and perform there in order to allow the two leaders to use the inside space of the circle. Some groups choose to enhance the percussive sounds further with one or two drums. Some drummers even take the liberty of improvising on top of the percussion patterns performed by the galombang members. In the pure traditional style, however, the percussion is created solely by the silek dancers.

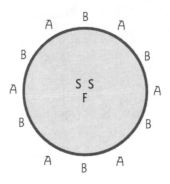

FIGURE 3: Circular group formation in a choral tapuak sequence
For choral tapuak sequences, the galombang members split into
two groups, here indicated by A and B. The two singers (S)
and the flute player (F) stand in the center.

Randai, Silek, and the Minangkabau Culture

Silek has played an important role in the emergence and development of Randai. It seems virtually certain that Randai evolved out of silek via the circular martial arts dance called *dampeang*, which was customarily employed in silek training and which was accompanied by music and songs that related simple stories. In the process of the development of Randai, the movement and songs became more complex. Other elements like storytelling, additional folk songs, and acting were adapted and integrated to create this unique composite performance art of the Minangkabau.

The current performance features bear witness to the important role of silek in the evolution and development of Randai. The percussive patterns performed by the galombang dancers derive from specific slapping techniques used in silek which have been developed into a complex and exciting musical feature of

Randai. The spatial arrangement of the galombang derives directly from the circular formation of the dampeang martial arts dance. The movement repertoire of the fighting scenes and the galombang in Randai derives from the prevalent local style of silek. In the fighting scenes, standard jurusan are modified slightly to render them more theatrical. Moreover, to enhance the dramatic nature of these fighting scenes, jurusan are often arranged in order of increasing difficulty and complemented with acrobatics and acting. The galombang is based on silek movement and often incorporates jurusan. These are modified and arranged into a circular group formation. Due to this formation—as well as the repetition, simultaneity, and the synchronization of these movements with the music and vocal cues from the circle leader—the galombang takes on a dance-like quality. Its foundation, however, is silek.

Randai is certainly not the only Asian theatre form that incorporates martial arts. Javanese *wayang wong*, Balinese *gambuh*, Indian *kathakali*, Beijing opera, and many others utilize martial arts to various degrees in a theatrical context. Randai, however, is special in that it evolved directly out of silek; the "flowering of silek" became Randai. One can speculate on why these two forms are so intricately linked. Certainly silek itself is practiced as a kind of performance art. Although it is primarily an art of self-defense and a way to train one's body and mind, "training sessions" are frequently performed publicly and take on the aesthetic qualities of a performance art. Costuming and music are an integral part of silek as well, and so too are the dance-like opening sequences and the circular practice formation.

Silek is a core element of the Minangkabau culture. Indeed, its importance can hardly be overemphasized. Even the smallest hamlet has its own silek school, and every young boy obtains some basic training. Silek is very much ingrained in the culture, and its philosophy—preserved in proverbs—permeates many other aspects of social life. This can be illustrated by the fact that the art of storytelling (*bakaba*) features silek thematically in its story material. Local folk heroes featured in this oral literature are without exception silek masters; combat scenes are vividly related in this still popular art form; silek-related proverbs abound. Silek is ever-present in the Minangkabau social fabric, therefore, it seems natural for such an important element of the culture to be nurtured into a full-fledged theatrical form. Today Randai itself continues to "flower" and is modified and adapted to evolving sociocultural changes. The martial arts, however, remain at its core.

Notes

[1] *Dampeang* (or *dampeng*) is first referred to in an 1891 Dutch dictionary (Toorn, 1891). It is described as a circular martial arts dance accompanied by singing and hand-clapping. Interestingly, the name is used interchangeably with the term Randai. Consequently, the term *Randai* was used to describe a circular martial arts dance accompanied by music before it developed into its current dramatic form.

[2] Other theories claim that storytelling or song/dance are the root of Randai (Pauka, 1996: 18–20). Since the first record of a Randai performance in its current dramatic form dates from 1932 (Nor, 1986: 18), no details about its emergence prior to this date are known for certain. The silek theory is supported by local scholars as well as by Randai and silek practitioners (Harun, 1992; Zulkifli, 1993; Kartomi, 1981).

[3] Dampeang in Pariaman is based on the local martial art styles, mainly *Ulu Ambek* and *Silek Mangguang*. Ulu Ambek itself is one of the more mystical and secretive styles and is featured in a ceremony called *Pauleh Tinggi*, a ritual event that occurs only in Pariaman and is put on about every twenty-five years (for a detailed description see *Journal of Asian Martial Arts* 4:3).

[4] This significant addition is vividly described by local artists. However, some scholars (Nor, 1986) maintain that impersonation was not part of Randai until the Malay bangsawan comedy theatre became popular in West Sumatra and gave the impetus to incorporate acting into the (until then nondramatic) Randai.

[5] Kartomi mentions that by the late 1970s female Randai actresses and singers existed: "In most villages, however, women do not take part in Randai performances; men still normally play all the female roles" (Kartomi, 1981: 23). In 1994, less than twenty years later, almost all groups featured female performers, not only as actresses and singers, but even as silek and dance performers.

[6] This origin theory is also supported by the etymology of the word *Randai*. The name *Randai* was associated with the circular martial arts dance (interchangeably with *dampeang*) as early as 1891 and possibly much earlier, before complex stories (*kaba*) or dramatic elements were incorporated. The term *Randai silek* is still used today to describe the circular practice formation employed in the martial arts. Moreover, the word *Randai* is believed to have derived from *berhandai-handai*, that is, "to be intimate, be friends with," a concept central to the group practice of silek (Harun, 1992: 72). Another theory surrounding this word traces its meaning to *baRandai*, that is, "to dance in a circle," also lending credibility to the theory that movement, not storytelling, was the starting point of Randai.

7　It is interesting to note that bangsawan has also influenced the development of other popular theatre forms in Indonesia, for instance, *sandiwara* in Sunda.

8　*Saluang jo dendang* (flute and song) predated Randai and constituted another main influence in the development of Randai toward its present form. More and more female singers started to sing in Randai, replacing or complementing the male singers, and bringing with them a new repertoire of melancholy love songs. Once women were part of the company, the move from singing to acting in the female roles became plausible. In this manner, dendang singers are believed to have become the first female actresses in Randai.

9　As singers rarely participate in the scenes or dances, they need not be proficient in silek.

10　This is a recurrent feature of other Indonesian theatre forms as well, for instance, *wayang kulit* and *wayang wong*.

11　*Maelo rambuik dalam tapuang* literally means "pulling a hair out of the flour." It is a Minangkabau idiom that refers to solving a problem diplomatically—like carefully pulling a hair from a bag of flour without breaking the hair or spilling the flour.

12　The custom of arranged marriages—commonly arranged by the maternal uncles (*mamak*)—is part of the Minangkabau culture. Randai stories often feature the problems resulting from such forced marriages.

13　The orchestra consists of the *talempong* (five bronze kettles) and several drums and flutes.

14　There is some flexibility in terms of how many and which jurusan are selected for a performance. But within each jurusan the movement sequence is set. The example cited here shows one variation of the fighting scene performed by this group. In other performances I saw longer versions which included two or more additional jurusan.

15　This is also true for silek practice sessions. In real applications—that is, in self-defense situations—any of the displayed techniques would be executed to maim or immobilize an attacker. In Randai, as in silek practice sessions, the fighters allow each other to escape from a hold or pin in order to continue the practice/performance. This would not be the case, of course, in a self-defense situation.

16　The design of these Randai pants also stems from silek pants; the only difference is that Randai pants have an even lower crotch. The extra fabric can be stretched by spreading the legs; when hit, it produces a loud drumlike sound.

17　Advanced performers do this even while jumping.

18　In performance this subtlety often gets drowned out by the crowds, thus it is more likely to be heard in the somewhat less noisy rehearsals.

[19] For a detailed notation of the main percussive tapuak patterns used in Randai see Pauka (1995b: 140–150). The notation used there is based on the time unit box system (TIBS) (Koetting, 1970: 125).

Bibliography

Alexander, H., et al. (1970). *Pentjak silat: The Indonesian fighting art*. Rutland, VT: Charles E. Tuttle.

Cordes, H. (1990). Pencak silat: Die kampfkunst der Minangkabau und ihr kulturelles umfeld. Doctoral dissertation, University of Cologne, Germany.

Draeger, D., & Smith, R. (1969). *Comprehensive Asian fighting arts*. Rutland, VT: Charles E. Tuttle.

Draeger, D. (1972). *Weapons and fighting arts of the Indonesian archipelago*. Rutland, VT: Charles E. Tuttle.

Errington, F. (1984). *Manners and meaning in West Sumatra*. New Haven: Yale University Press.

Echols, J., & Shadily, H. (Eds.). (1990). *Indonesian-English dictionary*. 3rd ed. Jakarta: Gramedia.

Harun, C. (1992). *Kesenian Randai di Minangkabau*. Jakarta: Depdikbud.

Kartomi, M. J. (1981). Randai theatre in West Sumatra: Components, music, origins, and recent change. *Review of Indonesian and Malay Affairs 15*(1), 1–45.

Maadis, I. (14 March 1988). Proses kelahiran Randai. *Harian Haluan* (Pandang), p. 6.

Murad, A. (1980). *Merantau: Outmigration in a matrilineal society of West Sumatra*. Canberra: Australian National University Press Service.

Nor, M. (1986). *Randai dance of Minangkabau Sumatra with labanotation scores*. Kuala Lumpur: Department of Publications, University of Malaysia.

Pauka, K. (1995a). Martial arts, magic, and male bonding: The pauleh tinggi ceremony of West Sumatra. *Journal of Asian Martial Arts 4*(3), 26–45.

Pauka, K. (1995b). Conflict and combat in performance: An analysis of the Randai folk theatre of the Minangkabau in West Sumatra. Doctoral dissertation with CD-ROM, University of Hawai'i.

Phillips, N. (1981). *Sijobang: Sung narrative poetry of West Sumatra*. New York: Cambridge University Press.

Toorn, J. L. v. d. (1891). *Minangkabausch-Maleisch-Nederlandsch Woordenbök*. The Hague: Martinus Nijhoff.

Zulkifli, A. (1993). Randai sebagai teater rakyat Minangkabau di Sumatera barat dalam dimensi sosial budaya. Unpublished thesis, Padang Panjang: ASKI.

Silat-Based Randai Theatre
of West Sumatra
Makes Its U.S. Debut
by Kirstin A. Pauka, Ph.D.

Photos courtesy of Kirstin Pauka. Those showing
the theatre performance were taken by Tom Levy.

Introduction

Silat is the indigenous martial art found throughout Malaysia and Indonesia, with myriad regional styles of great diversity. The silat style found in West Sumatra as practiced by the Minangkabau ethnic group is also called *silek* in the Minang language, and has twelve recognized major regional styles (Pauka, 1986a & b). *Randai* theatre, the indigenous Minangkabau theatre form, is fundamentally based on silat techniques and aesthetics. Besides martial arts, Randai features dance, acting, singing, instrumental music, and a unique type of percussion played by the dancers on their pants while dancing. Randai training and performance are community-centered activities, based symbolically and also quite literally on a circle. Randai's main functions in the village community are education and entertainment. Spiritual aspects central to silat training also carry over into Randai training and performance, especially into the structure of the learning process and into the relationships between teachers and students.

This article focuses on the use of silat training in Randai theatre as it was experienced in the US for the first time, during an extended artist-in-residence

45

program in the Asian Theatre Program at the University of Hawai'i. For this six-month program, two West Sumatra master artists were resident in the Theatre and Dance Department to train students in silat and Randai: Musra Dahrizal,[2] Randai artist and silat master; and Hasanawi,[3] Minangkabau music expert. The intensive training period culminated in the first-ever English language performances of Randai in the US in February 2001.

Silat and Randai Training
in the Asian Theatre Program
at the University of Hawai'i

The University of Hawai'i Asian Theatre Program has a long history of hosting distinguished Asian performing artists for lengthy residencies during which theatre, dance, and music students learn a specific Asian dance-drama genre in intensive 6–12 month training programs. The training process culminates in public performances of an Asian play in English, such as Japanese Kabuki, Chinese Xingqu, Balinese Kecak, and Indian Sanskrit plays. Over the years, many of these productions have included fighting scenes based on traditional martial arts from the individual region.

In the academic year 2000–2001, the Asian theatre genre selected for this program was a "historical first": Sumatran Randai. The training and production program of this Randai faced many unique challenges. A Randai play had never been done in English in the US, had rarely been learned by non-Indonesian students, and almost never been seen by a Western audience. The guest artists were traditional folk practitioners, who had never taught in a US university system, and had never taught foreign students. In addition, Randai is strongly based in martial arts and thereby poses additional challenges in terms of high physical demands on the students and the underlying spiritual and often mystical teachings. How would Western students absorb and modify this "foreign" form?

In the last decade, cross-cultural exchanges between Asian and US theatre artists and multicultural productions and workshops have become commonplace in the US and abroad. Along with this proliferation, questions about true cross-cultural learning and cross-cultural understandings and misunderstandings are being raised. How can one tailor and guide the complex process of learning a foreign theatre or martial arts genre? How do we translate language, customs, cultural values, spiritual teachings, musical conventions, and theatrical expression so that the process is mutually beneficial for participants, teachers, and audiences, and also create performances with high production standards?

46

In the case of silat and Randai training, the spiritual connection that was established between the teachers and students was, in my opinion, one of the main reasons for the project's success. The thorough grounding in silat's practice and spiritual teachings offered the students a vital and direct link to the essence of Randai. For instance, cleansing ceremonies that were done for the cast members by silat master Musra Dahrizal were crucial points in the development of the group into true *anak Randai* (children of Randai). With this, the "circle" of the new Randai community became a living reality for the students. The connection between teachers and students became those of master and apprentice in the full sense of the word.

Besides the silat training and spiritual essence underlying Randai, how is silat actually incorporated into a Randai performance? All the circular *galombang* dances are based on basic silat steps and gestures, but they are clearly choreographed and executed in time to the musical accompaniment of the orchestra and singers, thereby becoming more dance-like. In addition, pure fighting sequences are frequently included in those dances, typically at the end of a sung verse. These *jurusan* sequences consist of set attack-defense moves with punches, kicks, counterpunches, kicks, locks, and escapes, most frequently executed by all dancers arranged in pairs. Most basic silat maneuvers find their way into jurusan at some point in the play. Most plays feature at least one major fighting scene, part of which is generally choreographed, and part of which is free fighting, depending on the performers' skill level. Our story actually featured a sub-plot in which the main hero, Umbuik Mudo, goes off to study with a famous silat teacher, thereby giving ample opportunity to feature actual silat training sessions and silat competitions as part of the play.

As we have seen, silat is the basis for all movement, rhythm, and aesthetic in Randai theatre; therefore, basic silat training is mandatory for all Randai performers. In the University of Hawai'i production, all cast members (actors, dancers, and even musicians) had to participate in basic silat training. Basic silat steps and attack-defense sequences (*jurusan*) were taught to the dancers and actors in preparation for the movements and fighting sequences of the dance sequences central in Randai performances, called *galombang*. Additional, more advanced training sessions were held for those actors who performed longer fighting scenes. The photos below show examples of several basic silat steps as well as more advanced combinations of defense moves from the Silek Tuo style that were part of the silat training at the University of Hawai'i.[4]

Documentation of Silat Techniques

SECTION I
Examples of single-handed defenses against single strikes

Basic single-handed attacks can be countered either via the inside or outside of the attacking arm, with a same-side block or a cross block. All blocks usually have multiple follow-up options. The photos below show a few of those possibilities.

Photo 1: The attacker on the left (student) attacks with a straight punch to the solar plexus. The defender (Musra Dahrizal) uses a single-handed block to the inside of the attacker's wrist, while simultaneously stepping off the line of attack to the inside.

Photo 2: Same attack. The defender uses a single-handed cross-block to the inside of the attacker's wrist and grabs the wrist for a follow-up technique.

Photos 3a, b, c: Same attack. The defender uses a single-handed block to the outside of the attacker's wrist, and grabs it in preparation for follow-up techniques. A quick shuffle step closes the gap to the attacker, the initial wrist grab remains in place while the defender readies his other arm for an elbow strike to the opponent's elbow (3b), or chin (3c).

SECTION 2
Examples of double-handed defenses against single strikes

Photo 4a, b, c: Following a single-handed attack, the defender grabs and twists the wrist with both hands. Applying pressure to the joint through twisting and pressing inward (4b), he forces his opponent to the ground. An optional follow-up to this take-down is a shuffle step to close the gap and a combination of neck twist and knee strike to the opponent's elbow.

Photos 5a, b: Following a single-handed grab attack, the defender (the student) rotates her hand forward and out to twist the attacker's arm, then moves in to apply pressure to the outside of the attackers elbow which leads to a take-down. Notice the teacher's set-up for another counterattack by lodging his foot behind the heel of the student from where he could execute a leg sweep and reverse the wrist lock on her. Ideally, advanced practitioners can continue to "play" (*main terus*) countering each counterattack again and again, which can go on for a time, using variations of the basic wrist, elbow, and shoulder locks to unbalance their training partner.

Photo 6

Instead of moving to the elbow for the take-down as demonstrated in Photo 5b, the teacher shows another option here: by applying pressure to the back of the student's shoulder joint, he can unbalance her and achieve a similar but lower take-down.

SECTION 3
Examples of defenses against kicks

Photo 7: The attacker on the right (student) attacks with a straight kick. The defender catches the foot and applies pressure to the toes, unbalancing the opponent.

Photo 8: Same attack. The defender steps off the line of attack toward the inside, catches the foot with both hands, and applies pressure to the inside of the foot, forcing the opponent to rotate and lose balance.

Photo 9: A variation to the technique shown in Photo 8. Here, the second hand applies pressure to the knee instead of to the side of the foot, in preparation for a take-down.

Photo 10: Same attack. The defender steps off the line to the outside, catches the foot with both hands, and applies pressure to the outside of the foot, with a similar effect as in Photo 8.

Photo 11a, b: A variation of the defense from the outside. Here the second hand applies pressure to the knee instead of the side of the foot, with the same result as in Photo 9. Shown here is the follow-up take-down that results from the continued pressure applied to the side of the knee.

SECTION 4
Examples of kick defenses against single-handed strikes

Photo 12: Attacker (right) strikes with a straight punch to the solar plexus. The defender quickly moves off to the outside and checks the attacker's arm at the elbow. A possible follow-up here is to kick the elbow, resulting in the attacker losing balance.

Photo 13: The same technique as in Photo 12, except that the defensive kick is applied to the inside of the attacker's elbow.

SECTION 5

Examples of double defenses against double attacks (hand and foot)

Photo 14: Double outside cross-block with hand and foot, crossing at the wrist and ankle respectively. This technique is often used in basic exercises during which the students move backwards and forwards across the floor, retaining the proper fighting distance. As a defense, it sets up any number of follow-up techniques, similar to single-handed attacks.

Photo 15: The attacker punches and kicks simultaneously, the defender (right) blocks the kick to the outside with the hand (hidden from view behind the teacher's thigh) and uses a one-handed defense against the punch, similar to single-hand defenses, here with an inside variation of the wrist grab.

Photo 16: The attacker kicks and simultaneously executes a knifehand strike to the temple. The defender enters inside with a body turn that allows him to catch the leg, while at the same time extending the other hand for a counter-strike to the throat. This is a difficult technique only taught to students at the intermediate level.

Photo 17: Same attack. The defender moves to the outside with a body twist, and catches the leg and arm together to immobilize the attacker. Like the technique in Photo 16, this is also an advanced technique. Both are executed rapidly and depend on accurate timing so that the opponent's leg can be caught before the kick is retracted.

SECTION 6
Examples of advanced head-hold techniques

Photo 18: An advanced head-twisting technique is applied as a counterattack to the high foot-locking technique shown in photo 17. Both hands twist the head to one side, forcing the opponent to release the hold on the leg.

Photo 19: A similar head-twisting technique is used against a similar hold on the foot, here at a lower level than in photo 18.

Photo 20: A head-locking technique is applied as a defense against a kick. The head-lock here is the follow-up technique to a quick evasive move in which the defender jumps to the other side of the attacker, thereby evading the kick, and unbalancing the opponent.

Photo 21: Another example of an evasive move to a punch brings the defender (left) behind the attacker from where he can execute a controlling head-lock.

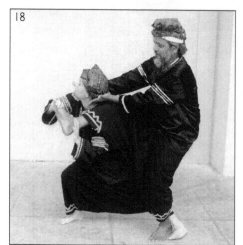

SECTION 6
Silat in Randai performance

The following photos show examples of silat elements in Randai performance.

Photo 22: The opening formation of a Randai performance is often done in lines that later spread out into a circle. Here, the performers enter in three lines. Once in place, the dancers perform a fast-paced silat sequence. The dancers from both outside lines alternatingly attack the dancers in the center line. This creates an exciting opening number and sets a lively mood for what follows.

Photo 23: The basic circle formation of a Randai performance. The dancers move counterclockwise around the circle using silat steps, turns, and hand gestures, accompanied by a song and flute piece.

Photo 24: Circle formations can be doubled, with an inner and outer circle for variety. The dancers here perform the signature technique of Randai, the percussive pants-slapping while dancing (*tapuak*).

Photo 25:
A close-up of silat steps as done during the *galombang* dance in preparation of an attack-defense sequence with a partner.

Photo 26—29: These photos show various silat elements of the jurusan sequences, attack-defense sections done by all dancers simultaneously and in time to the circle leader's vocal cues.

Photo 26: A straight punch is countered by a grab and elbow strike.

Photo 27: A double kick is executed by both dancers simultaneously, and countered by one of them with an open-handed block (hidden from view behind the left dancer's thigh).

Photo 28 and 29: A straight kick is countered by a grab and knee twist. This leads to the take-down (in 28) of the dancer on the right. She then counters with a backwards kick, a recovering step backwards, followed by a double elbow strike.

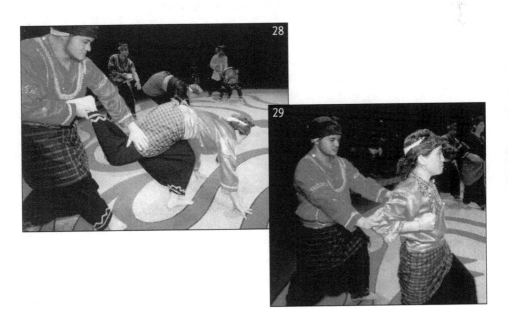

Photos 30 and 31: Fighting sequences are part of the acting in Randai and constitute a prominent feature of Randai theatre. In photo 30, the silat master teacher demonstrates a sequence during dress rehearsal. Photo 31: Both actors engage in a choreographed fighting scene during a performance.

Notes

[1] Musra Dahrizal, a native of Padang Panjang, West Sumatra, is a well-known traditional Minangkabau artist and an expert in silat, flute (*saluang*) music, and Randai theatre. Since 1991, he has been leading the Randai group "Palito Nyalo," one of the foremost Randai groups in West Sumatra today. Currently, he is also leading the "Rambun Sati" group. Besides actively practicing and teaching silat and Randai, Dahrizal is also a highly sought after saluang and dendang singing performer; he has recorded seven audio cassettes of saluang music.

[2] Like many Indonesians, Hasanawi goes by only one name. A native of Batusangkar, West Sumatra, he is a master teacher of traditional Minangkabau music, especially saluang, and other wind instruments like *bansi* and *sarunai*, as well as *gendang* drums and the traditional Minangkabau bronze percussion (*talempong*). This music is also used to accompany silat practice and performance. Silat students are expected to learn this music as well.

[3] These examples are by no means intended as a complete overview of Silek Tuo techniques of the Minangkabau, which is far beyond the scope of this article.

Additional Reading

Pauka, K. (1986a). Silek: The martial arts of the Minangkabau in West Sumatra. *Journal of Asian Martial Arts*, 6(1), 62–79.

Pauka, K. (1986b). A flower of martial arts: The Randai folk theatre of the Minangkabau in West Sumatra. *Journal of Asian Martial Arts*, 6(4), 10–29.

Silat Seni Gayong:
Seven Levels of Defense
by Mark V. Wiley

Photo illustrations courtesy of Sheikh Shamsuddin.

Conceived as an art of war, *Silat Seni Gayong* reflects the beliefs of an ancient culture and the concept of prevention. Developed in Malaya during the eleventh century, Silat Seni Gayong is an art of stopping wars, not creating them. It is one of preventing violence, not curing it.

In a discussion of Silat Seni Gayong's defensive techniques, more than mere physical movements must be addressed. In fact, there are seven areas of development that are primary constituents of Silat Seni Gayong defense.

1) Prevention of Conflict

Steeped in the religion of Islam, Malay silat teaches one to lead a life with great care so as not to provoke negative feelings from another, which, in turn, might spark a conflict. Islamic faith binds the culture of Malaysia with the deadly art of silat. Since Malaysian culture dictates a mutual respect for all, the best *pesilat* (silat disciple) is the most humble of persons.

According to the pesilat, the best means of self-defense is simply not to be in a position of having to defend oneself. The qualities that bring this belief to life are found in the prayer that is recited at the outset of every silat class. The prayer begins: "In the name of God, most gracious, most merciful." The attribute of being "most gracious" is the first quality a pesilat must possess. Proper respect must be held for man, the greatest of God's creations.

The second quality is being "most merciful." The pesilat must never abuse the privilege of using his art as that would be in a direct breach of trust with the Creator, for it is He who is truly most gracious and most merciful, and it is He who has given the pesilat his skills.

The application of these qualities is found in the *bunga* or dance of silat. During this sequence of movements, the pesilat offers his hands in friendship to his adversary not once, but twice. If the opponent is still intent upon inflicting injury, the pesilat then displays grace in his movements as he shows mercy in turning away. This turning away is misleading in that he really never takes his eyes off his opponent, and although his back is turned, the pesilat is still in a position of superior defense. Only if, after this point, his adversary persists will the pesilat employ his skills of self-defense.

To effectively employ Silat Seni Gayong for self-defense one must have an understanding of coordinated body movement. *Sunnah wal jamaah*, meaning "team effort," is the highest form of coordinating the body for self-defense in silat. From the training of the bunga, the pesilat develops a solid foundation and a unity of mind and body. Silat Seni Gayong is founded on the concept of team-work. In order for a team to work efficiently and effectively, each member must answer to one person, i.e., the coach. The pesilat first learns to center himself and then proceeds to put his team together. His "team" consists of the five senses, the physical body, balance, speed, timing, and accuracy. The pesilat believes that all these attributes answer to him and that he answers to God. From unity between mind and body, strengths and weaknesses, and with God, comes true strength.

2) Avoidance

Elakan, or avoidance, is the second level of Silat Seni Gayong defense; it is the first level of physical contact. Again, the concept of avoidance is stressed. If the pesilat is attacked, he maintains the quality mercy and avoids the attack. The Seni Gayong pesilat believes that when one blocks one is, in fact, striking an opponent. At the second level of defense, this is unacceptable.

The pesilat is taught to avoid oncoming attacks through *lankah* silat, or footwork, and redirection of the opponent's offensive movement. In Silat Seni Gayong avoidance of an attack is achieved by stepping back and redirecting the oncoming force with one's arm. Hitting or counterattacking has still not been employed because at this second level of defense the pesilat continues to follow the first two principles of being gracious and merciful. As in the bunga, the pesilat has now given his opponent a second chance to reconsider his attack.

3) Blocking

Tangkis, or blocking, is employed at Silat Seni Gayong's third level of defense. At this point the concept of a counterattack is first displayed through blocking and striking methods. By employing blocking techniques the pesilat has not only reduced the force of the oncoming blow but has inflicted a sudden shock to his opponent. In Malay silat, all blocks are actually strikes to nerve centers. By redirecting the force of the attack and inflicting pain in only the area that is posing an immediate threat to the pesilat (i.e., the arm), he is still displaying mercy.

4) Combat

It is when all else has failed that Silat Seni Gayong condones the infliction of harm to another person. Because the pesilat has trained from the beginning to harmonize with himself, he is programmed to defend himself against multiple opponents at all times. Thus, the pesilat is not surprised at the hidden dangers of personal combat.

Silat combat begins with checking one's own circle: a critical area around one's body. After the pesilat has checked his circle he unites his team. From this unity comes harmony, awareness, and deception through movement. To keep the awareness of his circle the pesilat does not stare at his opponent, but looks away. When one stares, his focal point is one. If his focal point is one, he can be deceived by his opponent and thus lose awareness of his entire circle. By not staring, one's focal point is nowhere, yet everywhere. This is not peripheral vision but harmony with one's surroundings.

Since the pesilat believes that God has entrusted him with more than himself (i.e., silat skills), physical pain is not a deterrent because the body heals, and death is not losing because it is part of an ongoing journey. The world to a pesilat is merely a place of transition; once his time is called he boards the bus and travels on. Because death is not a deterrent, the pesilat is not afraid to fight for what is right even if it means losing his own life in the process.

5) Unseen Weapons

Weapons pose no threat to the Seni Gayong pesilat for he has trained extensively in their use. However, when involved in self-defense, it is one's concealed weapons which are the most dangerous to one's attacker. Since the natural weapons of the pesilat are God given (i.e., hand and feet), they can be used to kill and heal. When it comes to defending his country or loved ones, the pesilat holds nothing back; however the choice of how he uses his weapons is up to him. There is an old Malay saying: "Left hand, hospital; right hand, graveyard."

6) Mind and Heart

The most important attribute of Silat Seni Gayong is the ethical understanding of the pesilat's actions. The pesilat fears the outcome of being put in a position of having to employ his deadly skills. As a result of possessing and developing these God-given fighting abilities, the pesilat must always hold sacred the first two qualities of graciousness and mercy.

The mind and heart of the pesilat never separate. The mind controls the body, and the heart is his soul. Many people associate "mind and body" but Malay silat connects "mind and heart." In silat, the body (external) is believed to be controlled by the mind, while the feelings (internal) are controlled by the heart. When speaking of counterattack in Malay silat, one must distinguish between physical and emotional attacks and their respective countermeasures.

This distinction is the foundation of Silat Seni Gayong. If the mind is wrong from the beginning, then how can anything be right? Everything is performed and achieved step by step. If negativity is cultivated from the beginning, then the pesilat will be in constant conflict with himself. The biggest war is that which is fought within. If the pesilat can control the internal war, then the external poses no real threat to him. If one cannot first help himself, then he will not be able to help or heal those in need.

If the mind and heart are not in unison, nothing can work. Graciousness keeps the pesilat from being offensive in nature. That is why the stages of self-defense include prevention, avoidance, and redirection. To the pesilat it is better to deal with every confrontation with good intent rather than with bad, for "what goes around comes around."

Only by respecting oneself does one deserve respect from others. If the mind is negative, negative actions will result from the body following the mind. A negative action cannot produce a positive reaction. Thus, in the realm of defense, if the intention of the pesilat is negative, his movements and reactions will be ineffective. This follows the Chinese principle of yin/yang in that the relationship between mind and body, or internal and external (batin/zahi), must be nurtured together in silat training.

7) Acceptance of Fate

The final level of defense in Silat Seni Gayong is the acceptance of one's own fate. Since God gave him life and silat skills, the pesilat believes that it is only God who can take them away and that his life rests in His hands.

The pesilat accepts all. He is not just a student of silat but a disciple of God. A student only learns, but a disciple "fine tunes" himself. The pesilat is never one to provoke, but rather avoids all possible confrontations through positive thoughts and actions. As a rotated sphere eventually returns to its original alignment, the pesilat believes that if he creates a negative action it will come back to him tenfold.

These are Silat Seni Gayong's seven steps of self-defense. They describe a necessary progression when employing the art for self-defense. The name of the system itself describes a necessary progression of individual development. *Silat* is the art, *seni* is the act of fine tuning that art, and *gayong* is the spiritual development of the pesilat.

Some Technical Applications of Silat Seni Gayong

Descriptions by Michael A. DeMarco, Editor-in-Chief

The following photographs illustrate a variety of self-defense applications used against attacks made bare-handed or with weapons such as a knife or sword. Nine sequences are shown, each illustrating some of the characteristics of silat movements.

Kombat Sembilan Belas Combat Technique

1a) Sheikh steps forward to block an oncoming sword attack by catching the wrist of his opponent, while simultaneously striking the opponent's ribs. **1b)** By keeping the opponent's sword arm to the outside, Sheikh can use leverage to bend the top half of the attacker's body slightly back. Sheikh quickly withdraws and repositions himself, placing his right calf behind the opponent's right leg. Simultaneously his right hand moves upward toward the opponent's jaw. **1c)** The attacker's torqued body enables Sheikh to easily perform a backward sweep with his right leg in conjunction with fluid hand movements which bring the attacker quickly down to the ground. Note that Sheikh maintains contact with the opponent's jaw and the sword arm. In this position, he can put pressure on the attacker's wrist and/or elbow to make him drop the sword.

Combat Sembilan Combat Technique

2a) The attacker is about to throw a right punch at Sheikh's solar plexus. **2b)** Side-stepping while blocking and grabbing the attacker's sleeve, Sheikh delivers a kick with the side of his right foot to the back of his opponent's knee. **2c)** The attacker thus loses his balance, turning his back toward Sheikh from the force of the kick. This allows Sheikh to grab the jaw of his attacker and bend him backwards far enough to deliver a final blow to the exposed neck. **2d)** The final strike can be delivered by the hand or elbow.

Buah Tiga Fruition

3a) The attacker is about to throw a right punch at Sheikh's solar plexus. **3b)** Sheikh side-steps toward the attacker's right side, blocking with his left forearm, and continues to circle backward with his right leg. **3c)** Before the attacker can reposition himself, Sheikh encircles and firmly locks the attacker's right arm. **3d)** While maintaining pressure on the lock, he places a choke hold on the opponent with his left arm. **3e)** Note that both of Sheikh's hands interlock, effectively sealing the attacker's right arm and head in one locking maneuver. **3f)** In an attempt to relieve the excruciating pain inflicted by the hold on his upper body, the attacker instinctively leans backwards. This makes it easy for Sheikh to drop to one knee, thus bringing further pain to the attacker's lower back, causing him to fall to his knees in total submission.

Pentas Set Movements

4a) Sheikh executes a kick which is blocked and caught by his opponent. **4b)** The opponent attempts to break the knee by exerting force against the knee-cap while maintaining a firm hold on Sheikh's ankle. Sheikh neutralizes the attempted break by twisting his body, making his right knee point downward. This also causes the opponent to be pulled forward. **4c-d)** The opponent, now off-balance, also loses his grip on Sheikh's right leg. Sheikh immediately throws a back-kick with his left leg to the opponent's mid-section.

Combat Lima Belas Combat Technique

5a) The attacker steps in to deliver an overhead strike. **5b)** Sheikh crossblocks the incoming strike with his right hand and simultaneously grabs both shoulders of the attacker with his crossed hands. **5c)** Sheikh utilizes the rotational effect of his first block by drawing the opponent further into a spin with a push/pull technique executed with both hands as his body shifts forward. **5d)** Since the attacker is now off-balance from the spin, Sheikh strikes with his knee to the center of the attacker's back along the spinal column. **5e)** Sheikh places his right foot on the ground behind the opponent just as the opponent falls backward. While keeping a right-hand hold on the attacker's shoulder, Sheikh flows with the falling opponent to simultaneously execute a final strike. This strike is made as Sheikh's body weight drops. Note that his right forearm continues to exert pressure against the attacker's throat until the series of movements is completed.

Combat Duatuluh Combat Technique

6a) The attacker readies himself to step in and attack with his right hand. **6b)** As the attacker strikes, Sheikh shifts his weight to his right leg, allowing him to evade the strike. The shift also enables him to use the instep of his left foot to kick the attacker's knee causing him to spin slightly and lose his balance. **6c)** As the attacker falls backward, Sheikh steps closer with his left foot. **6d)** Before the opponent can regain his guard, Sheikh moves in with a finishing kick to the groin.

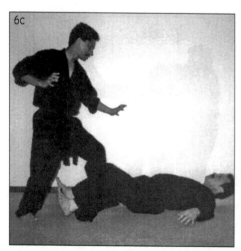

7a

7b

7c

7d

Combat Pisau Lima
Combat Knife Technique

7a) The attacker pretends to attack by raising his left hand, hoping to distract Sheikh and then make a deadly lunge with a knife concealed behind his right leg. **7b)** Sheikh blocks the strike at the attacker's wrist with his left hand as he steps backwards, but remains inside the circumference of the knife's path. He simultaneously delivers an open-hand blow to the attacker's temple. **7c)** Sheikh retreats to allow his right hand to slide into a two-handed grip around the attacker's right hand. This technique also aims at keeping the attacker's arm extended. By turning the wrist inward, Sheikh exherts pressure on the attacker's wrist, elbow and shoulder. The attacker instinctively bends forward in an attempt to relieve the pressure. **7d)** As the attacker bends forward, Sheikh delivers a powerful front kick to the mid-section. **7e)** The kicking leg immediately circles over the opponent's arm. The opponent's arm is easily broken at the elbow under the forces exerted by Sheikh's leg and grip.

7e

Kombat Pisau Enam Combat Knife Technique

8a) Sheikh cross-blocks an underhand knife attack. Although he steps backwards with his left leg, he keeps his weight on the front leg during the blocking technique. **8b)** A twisting technique immediately flows out of the cross-block which places pressure on the attacker's wrist, elbow and shoulder. The attacker instinctively bends forward in an attempt to relieve the pressure. **8c)** Sheikh wraps his left leg around the attacker's arm. He uses his own leg as leverage to fold the attacker's arm. This places the knife hand near the center of the attacker's back. The resulting pressure on the attacker's arm and wrist cause him to loosen his grip on the knife. **8d)** Sheikh grabs the knife as he drops his weight onto the attacker, who is already leaning forward. The attacker, with his right arm still in the leg lock, lies motionless under Sheikh's weight. Note the wrist lock Sheikh uses to maintain a high level of pain in the arm of his now weaponless attacker.

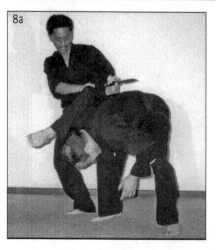

Kombat Pisau Tujuh Combat Knife Technique

9a) An attacker lunges forward with a knife. While stepping backwards and turning his body ninety degrees, Sheikh catches the wrist of the attacker. In this position, he directly faces the knife hand. **9b)** He delievers an open-hand strike directly to the attacker's wrist at such an angle that the knife is flung downward by the blow. **9c)** Not letting go of the attacker's right arm, Sheikh immediately follows with a kick to the stomach. **9d)** While the attacker bends forward in response to being kicked, Sheikh ends the sequence with a palm strike to the attacker's head.

Acnowledgment

Thanks to Randy Stigall for
assisting in the demonstrations.

71

Practical Fighting Strategies of Indonesian Kuntao-Silat in the Willem Reeders Tradition

by Michael DeMarco, M.A.

Grand Master Willem Reeders.
Photograph courtesy of Robert Servideo.

Introduction

What fighting arts are found in Indonesia? Do they have distinguishing traits that we can recognize as unique to that geographic area? Since the Republic of Indonesia is a country that comprises 17,508 islands and is home to over 230 million people, we can be certain there are numerous styles to bewilder any researcher. However, when looking at the variety of Asian martial art styles, there are a few characteristics that may help us distinguish which are Indonesian. Helpful guidelines can be derived from historical and geographical perspectives as well as combative body postures that seem to have been molded by centuries of social norms.

The following pages offer a very brief look at Indonesia's historical development and general features that may have contributed to its unique repertoire of martial art styles. The present understanding among the average reader is limited by the lack of publications about Indonesian martial arts, as well as the scarceness of qualified teachers living outside Indonesia. One important pioneer in bringing Indonesian martial arts to the United States was Willem A. Reeders (1917–1990).

This short article is a very humble attempt to present aspects of Reeders's teachings as indicators of the general state of Indonesian martial arts, how and why they are taught, and the general curricula. A technical section illustrates not only fighting techniques, but also the physical and mental traits that have permeated Indonesian culture in general.

Historical Elements in Indonesian Martial Arts

The world's fourth-most-populous country is blessed with abundant natural resources and has been a center of international trade for over two thousand years. Many ethnic groups came into contact with varying degrees of social mixing. Immigrants from India and China made major cultural contributions to Indonesia. For example, Buddhism and Hinduism mixed with native animism (Wilson, 1993). Muslims from India brought their religion also. Today the country is home to the largest Muslim population in the world. Many immigrants came to work and a large number became leading merchants. Of course, those with financial power played a growing part in the area's local and regional politics.

Europeans were drawn to Indonesia for the spice trade during their "Age of Discovery." The Portuguese were first, arriving in 1512, and the British and Dutch soon followed. The Dutch came to dominate much of the area now known as Indonesia from 1603 to 1949. It wasn't until World War II that circumstances ended Dutch rule. Since Japan invaded and occupied Indonesian islands during the war, and The Netherlands had to focus its energies on postwar rebuilding at home, the resulting strains forced the Dutch to eventually recognize Indonesian independence.

The brief overview presented above indicates the complex nature of Indonesian society. In all, there are over 300 ethnic groups in Indonesia that have contributed to a multicolored cultural tapestry. The resulting fabric possesses a mesmerizing beauty, but also includes inherent tensions stemming from social diversity among the numerous ethnic, cultural, and linguistic groups. Warfare and social disturbances have occurred across the lengthy archipelago in different times and locations over the centuries. Within each social layer the presence of martial arts can be found.

Research on Kuntao-Silat

Cimande, Pencak Silat, Bakti Negara, Cikalong, Harimau, Serak ... a long list of terms can describe Indonesian martial art styles. Some styles were named after particular masters, animals, locations, or associated combat terms. Major styles have branches, and branches have offshoots. The easiest way to classify Indonesian martial arts is to demarcate them into the two main categories: 1) *silat*: the indigenous martial arts, and 2) *kuntao* (Mandarin, *quandao*; "fist/boxing ways"): styles of Chinese origin.

Immigrants from China came to Indonesia over many centuries. Some Chinese fled to Southeast Asia as northern Chinese dynasties brought their power into southern China. Others came for work opportunities, and many became leading businessmen and traders. The waves of immigrants included boxing masters, a number of whom were enticed by wealthy merchants to teach Chinese and help protect their business establishments. There are still strong social ties among Chinese-Indonesians; however, social relations between them and native Indonesians remain strained to this day.

Kuntao styles bear resemblance to a number of styles from the Chinese mainland, especially those from the south, such as Shaolin styles of White Crane, Five Animals, etc. Time has allowed Chinese and native Indonesians to build better relationships—through friendships, intermarriages, and business relationships. In turn, this affected the martial arts' development with pure Chinese styles mixing in varying degrees with native Indonesian styles.

Reeders with his uncle, Liu Siong.
Photo courtesy of R. Lopez.

Native Indonesians also had a longstanding need to protect their interests, and martial arts permeated their culture from the village level up. Their styles are greatly influenced by ancient animistic beliefs and practices, along with complementary Hindu and Arab beliefs and practices (Wilson, 1993; Farrer, 2009). The resulting cultural blending can be seen in the number of physical arts, especially in dance and theatre (Pauka, 1986, 1998, 1999, 2003).

Many combative postures are low to the ground, in part because it is likely that combat would take place on slippery terrain. Indonesia is situated along the equator and is nearly all tropical with long monsoon seasons. Fighting on slippery terrain would necessitate that combatives styles include practical postures allowing one to fight on the ground, as well as provide a flowing continuity between ground and standing postures and vice versa (Davies, 2000). Low postures and ground fighting skills are also practical elements in kuntao-silat's fighting strategy.

Regarding Indonesian martial arts as an academic subject, books and articles of scholarly quality have been sorely lacking, especially compared with martial traditions of China, Japan, and Korea. Indonesian fighting arts have been secretive for centuries, and only in recent decades have there been substantial recordings made on film, in print, and in digital formats. In the early 1970s, Draeger, Alexander, and Chambers presented a glimpse into the martial arts of the archipelago through their books in English. However, no doubt because of the Dutch period of colonization, some of the best writings on kuntao-silat have been published by Europeans who have studied and lived in Indonesia. For example, Dr. Hiltrud Cordes wrote her doctorate dissertation (1990) on *pencak silat*. Dr. Kirstin Pauka's dissertation (1999) on Randai theatre was published in CD-ROM format, and she was responsible for the U.S. debut of silat-based Randai theatre of West Sumatra (2003). A recent example is Dr. Douglas Farrer's scholarly work dealing with the Muslim Sufi mysticism and silat (2009).

Of course, there is a growing amount of writings on websites about kuntao-silat, but most of it is presented for promotional reasons and is lacking in objectivity and accuracy. Oftentimes materials presented take the reader further from the truth than closer to it!

Migration and the Spread of Kuntao-Silat

There is a large number of martial art practitioners spread throughout the Indonesian archepeglago. A relative number are highly skilled, but their names may not be well-known outside their own locale. For fame and honor, there were formerly regular challenge matches, often including weapons. Some masters have gained reputations much like gunfighters in the American "Wild West." Over the centuries, fighting traditions were passed from generation to generation, usually within a family lineage or within a clan. Such arts continue to prosper today under similar conditions, while others are taking the modern route of commercializing kuntao-silat, bringing a few masters international acclaim.

Recent decades have seen a growth of kuntao-silat schools and associations in Indonesia. Ties established during the colonial period between the Netherlands and Indonesia contributed to the introduction and slow-growing presence of kuntao-silat in the Netherlands, where it later was spread into neighboring countries. However, by the mid-20th century, it was still very rare to see any martial art style from Indonesia performed publically outside the archipelago. Writings on Indonesian styles were rare. What could be better to gain knowledge of kuntao-silat than seeing a master in action? Some practitioners began presenting their arts to the public, and taking on students.

A few Dutch-Chinese kuntao-silat practitioners from Java emmigrated to the United States in the late 1950s and early 1960s, including Willem Reeders (1917–1990); three brothers, Paul de Thouars (1930–1972), Willem de Thouars (b. 1936), and Victor de Thouars; and Willy Wetzel (1921–1975). Their teachings and presentations brought some recognition of kuntao-silat to people in the United States and Canada.

Willem Reeders's Early Teachings in Western New York

The following pages focus on the teachings of Willem A. Reeders (1917–1990). He moved to the Jamestown, New York, area in the mid-1960s and to Albuquerque, New Mexico, in 1972, where he opened the doors to many new students. In the 1960s most people in the United States were aware of karate and judo, but little else of Asian martial traditions. Stylistically, Reeders's system was a stunning contrast to the karate styles popular during that period. An objective for this article is to look at Reeders's teaching and practice in order to gain one perspective on Indonesian fighting arts that may offer some insight into kuntao-silat systems in general.

Left: Willem Reeders. Right: Ernst Devries, Liu Siong,
and Willem Reeders practicing kuntao on the
island of Java. Photos courtesy of R. Lopez.

Reeders's teachings attracted a number of students from the Jamestown area at the far western corner of New York state. Jerry Bradigan was a longtime student who carries on Reeders's tradition in Fredonia, New York. Marilyn Feeney carries on his teaching in Albuquerque. Others studied with Reeders in Jamestown and also in Erie, Pennsylvania. Noted first-generation students from the Erie area include Raymond Cunningham (1928–2008), Arthur E. Sykes (1934–2008),

Richard Lopez (b. 1933), Harry Zimmerman, Ed "Tiny" Sealy, Ed Carter, and Robert Servidio. One of the most respected of Reeders's students is Mr. Servidio, noted for his highly advanced level in the system, as well as his upright character.

What did Reeders teach? Ask his longtime students and their answers vary. According to Reeders's students, his main influence came from his grandmother's brother, Liu Seong, who moved to Indonesia from China. Uncle Liu taught young Willem the family gongfu system. In addition, Reeders studied a number of kuntao and silat styles, plus Shotokan karate and Kodokan judo. From his rich trove of combat skills, he taught different techniques to different students, and changed curricula over time and locations.

Because many were familiar with Japanese martial art terminology, Reeders and students often mixed Japanese terms with unfamiliar Indonesian and Chinese terminology. Many students, unaware of Asian history and language, misinterpreted much. Intentionally or unintentionally, Reeders himself was responsible for passing on inaccuracies regarding the history of what he taught and where his techniques originated. To this day, second- and third-generation practitioners often repeat hearsay as fact, many times adding their own embellishments. Others note the inconsistencies, mistranslations of foreign terms, and hyperbole, and simply state that they cannot clearly separate the fact from the fiction.

What proves certain is that Willem Reeders taught a variety of styles. As a Dutch-Chinese living in Indonesia, his studies were primarily Chinese-based kuntao styles, but included training in native Indonesian silat styles as well. From his technical repertoire, he taught whatever he wanted. Students may not have known what style they were studying; all they knew was that Reeders was a superb fighter with something special to teach.

Robert Servidio, center, is flanked by his teacher and his top student, Scott Young, in Albuquerque, NM. *Photo courtesy of R. Servidio.*

Reeders with his uncle, Liu Siong.
Photo courtesy of Richard Lopez.

First-Generation Representatives: Arthur Sykes and Richard Lopez

In 1965 my introduction to the martial arts came through Arthur "Sonny" Sykes. My friend and classmate at the time was Thomas Pepperman, one of Sykes's most senior students. I worked out with Tom regularly for a few years. Classes with Mr. Sykes were never regular, but they were always insightful. This period was important for me because it brought a reality of what combatives were designed to do. Performed at a high level of skill, kuntao-silat is fluid, yet powerful and devastating. Practice was sweaty, interesting, and fun. I appreciated the gesture when Tom presented me a green belt, which was originally given to him by Sykes. Unfortunately, Sykes's classes were not always on a schedule, and became even more irregular.

On a warm summer day in 1971, I went to a car wash and needed change. I asked a guy if he had some quarters for a dollar bill. His name was Richard "Dick" Lopez, and he recognized my family name and knew my relatives. Turns out he was one of the earliest from the Erie area to study with Willem Reeders. When we met, Lopez was teaching kuntao-silat in a small studio behind the home of another Reeders student, ex-marine Raymond Cunningham (1928–2008). He invited me to visit his school.

As it turned out, Lopez was a gem of a martial artist and, more important, proved to be a man of rare character. I can call him a true friend for life. He began his studies with karate and judo in Erie, Pennsylvania. His judo skills benefited by studies in Germany while he was serving in the military. When he returned to the United States, he heard that Willem Reeders was teaching judo and karate in Jamestown, New York. Lopez went to meet him, was impressed with his judo, and traveled weekly to study with him. They developed a good friendship through their joy of judo practice and humor. When Reeders decided to stop teaching judo and start teaching kuntao, Lopez decided to study the new curriculum. Others followed Lopez to study with Reeders.

Reeders & Richard Lopez. • Lopez practicing with *tjabang*, early 1970s. He made many tjbang according to Reeder's stylistic specifications. *Photos courtesy of R. Lopez.*

Richard Lopez countering his student Peter Pjecha's knife thrust by utilizing kuntao principles. Early 1970s. *Photo courtesy of R. Lopez.*

Lopez would take my kuntao-silat studies to a higher level, but more important, he was a living example of what martial arts entailed, technically and theoretically. Although I chose not to wear any belts, he presented me with an orange sash (black belt level). The sash is valuable to me, not as any symbol of rank, but for what it specifically means coming from this person I respect. It represents a part of Lopez's own tradition.

Lopez was well trained. He would teach—showing what he learned and explaining where the techniques came from—but he always would point out the limits of what he was absolutely sure about regarding style, technique, and history.

Sykes and Lopez both studied closely with Reeders. When in Erie, Reeders often stayed at the Lopez home. As first-generation students, Sykes and Lopez eventually started teaching, and the methodology used was the same that Reeders taught them. Most classes focused on learning the movements in a technique and its application, and perhaps some variations. Students individually practiced the movements repetitively for most of the class time. The same techniques were later practiced with a partner, repeated for months until the techniques became fluid. Speed intensified and control became more and more precise. Few forms were taught, but there was a lot of sparring. Reeders was quite fluent with a variety of weapons, a favorite being the *tjabang* (Japanese, *sai*) (Dohrenwend, 2002). However, it seems he shared only part of his repertoire with selected students.

Lopez kept the same type of teaching regimen as Reeders, while Sykes changed over the years by embellishing whenever he liked. For example, he created a number of routines from the individual techniques he learned from Reeders. In "karate tournaments" during the 1960s, Sykes would state the kata's name—which he had just made up—and then spontaneously perform for judges. If asked to repeat the routine, of course he'd opt to perform a different one! Very creative.

Reeder's with Arthur Sykes, who became a leading representative of the system.

The common thread in Reeders's teachings—clearly exemplified through the way Sykes, Lopez, Cunningham, and Pepperman were teaching—is practicality. Theory and practice had one objective, which was to devastate an opponent or opponents as quickly and severely as possible. Lopez said Reeders often referred to his methods as "dirty fighting." There was nothing nice or compassionate about them. There was little pushing or restraining, but there were plenty of finger strikes to the eyes, throat, and groin areas. Blocks were usually not simply blocks, but were employed to break bone or cripple. Neck, vertebrae, and joints were targeted for quick breaks. Defense and attack blended into one concept where the mind and body moved spontaneously as needed.

Lopez instructing the author (*tjabang* / staff). Photo taken inside
Ray Cunningham's 80studio in the early 1970s. *Photo courtesy of R. Lopez.*

The following technical section presents a few examples of Reeders kuntao-silat as taught by Sykes and Lopez.

Technical Section

The goal for a kuntao-silat practitioner is to end any confrontation quickly. Combative encounters are not prolonged exhibitions of skills, as so commonly shown in the movie industry. Two fundamental guidelines for Indonesian systems are to evade any attack and to incapacitate the attacker. In most cases, one can evade an attack by moving the body away or turning at angles to deflect or neutralize the opponent's movement. Incapacitating an attacker is usually accomplished by attacking soft vital areas, such as the eyes, ears, throat, groin, and joints. Highly skilled masters evade and attack simultaneously at lightning speed.

Defenses Against a Front Kick — Stepping to the Outside

A1 The defender steps into an open guard position with his stance spread to the left and right. **A2** As the attacker kicks, the defender moves his right arm counterclockwise to circle under the kicking leg while shifting onto the left foot, turning the body, and bringing the right foot behind. (In full movement, catching the kicking leg in an upward movement will cause the attacker to lean backward.) Just as the right hand catches the kick's upward movement, the left arm moves clockwise to elbow strike, breaking the knee. **A3** An alternative to the above technique is to circle the right arm clockwise as the body shifts left and turns into the crouching posture. As the body sinks, the right backfist comes downward on the attacker's shin, making the attacker off balance and potentially fracture the tibia.

Defense Against a Punch — Stepping to the Outside

From an initial face-to-face standing position, the attacker throws a right punch. **B1** The defender steps with his left foot to the outside of the attacker's arm at a 45-degree angle while simultaneously blocking the attacking arm at the elbow and letting his right leg follow the 45-degree angle movement. The right foot does not touch the ground, but immediately reverses direction. **B2** As the right leg sweeps backward, the right palm swings upward to strike the attacker's jaw. Following through with the coordinated sweep and palm strike would cause the attacker to slam to the ground. The palm strike can break the neck.

Against a Punch

C1 The defender steps outside the line of attack, moving his right arm clockwise to meet the attacking arm with his forearm and smoothly sliding down to grasp the opponent's wrist. His left arm simultaneously follows to break the elbow.

C2 The defender immediately turns his body right, moving his left arm to his right side, then **C3** shifts toward the attacker with an elbow strike to the ribs, which **C4** causes the attacker to bend forward into a backfist.

Against a Punch

D1 The defender first steps outside the line of attack with his left foot and turns right, bringing his right hand circling down on the attacker's arm. **D2** The left arm follows the same circular path, sliding down the attacker's arm to secure the fist. The momentum pulls the attacker's head downward, and he instinctively draws his head upward, exposing his throat. **D3** The defender reverses movement, turning left and striking with his palm. **D4** He follows with a leg reap, which would cause a fall.

Defense Against a Punch — Stepping to the Inside

E1 The defender steps into an open guard position with his stance spread to the left and right. His weight is mostly on his left leg. **E2** As the attacker strikes, the defender shifts onto his right leg as he turns his waist left, bringing his right arm to circle toward his left shoulder, flowing with the incoming strike, but keeping it safely to the side. **E3** The right hand continues to circle slightly downward as the left arm circles upward against the attacker's arm. This frees the right hand to strike the attacker's face or eyes, causing the head to tilt backward. **E4** The left hand also continues to circle downward and flows into a midsection strike, **E5** followed by a palm strike to the groin **E6**.

Wrap Around

In the case of confronting multiple attackers, a simple guideline is to move where there is the least danger. **F1** An attacker readies to strike. The defender observes the surroundings. **F2** As the punch is executed, the defender steps slightly back and to the right side. **F3** Seeing another potential attacker approaching from the right, the defender swiftly moves to the left, underneath the striking arm. He thus uses the attacker as a barrier between himself and the other potential attacker. **F4** While he moves close to the attacker and turns his shoulders left, the momentum brings his left elbow into the attacker's midsection. **F5** The defender reverses direction to the right, bringing in another elbow strike to the attacker's back. **F6** While shifting slightly left, the defender turns his body right, letting his right foot pivot on the heel before stepping with his left foot behind the attacker. **F7-8** The defender then steps to the side with his right foot allowing a backfist strike, reverse, and leg reap.

Thoughts on Kuntao-Silat

At the start of this article, we asked what traits distinguish kuntao-silat from other Asian martial arts. The natural starting point for this inquiry is Indonesia's geographic setting as the crucible where kuntao-silat developed and where it was nurtured through contributions from three main cultures: 1) native, 2) Indian, and 3) Chinese. Considering that this archipelago includes hundreds of islands and many ethnic groups, there has been a history of strife at the village and regional levels for nearly two millennia. Over the centuries, the sociopolitical pressures among groups made martial art study a priority.

The ancient native culture included animistic beliefs and a physical regimen that suited the Southeast Asian body type and lifestyle in the equatorial tropics. Sufi mysticism from India, as well as Chinese Daoist beliefs, blended to give kuntao-silat unique psychological tools that infused their fighting arts. An example is how the mesmerizing music of a gamelan ensemble can enhance the hypnotic, deathly dance of a Pukulan silat practitioner. Actually, kuntao-silat is often practiced with musical accompaniment.

The practice of Chinese animal styles was animated by the very presence of dangerous and cunning animals living in the Indonesian jungles, such as the fierce sun bear, Komodo dragon, Sumatran tiger, and numerous species of snakes and monkeys. Chinese kuntao mixed with silat, and both no doubt were also tinged with theories and practices from India, such as the fighting art of kalarippayattu.

All people living on the Indonesian islands have blended a variety of cultural streams to form their own unique identities. Martial artists in Indonesia manifested their arts with differences, much the way that faces of members in one family reflect their own identities. Indonesian martial arts are largely individualistic hybrid styles containing elements of body movement found also in Indonesian-style dance and theatre.

When we look at any form of kuntao-silat, we see movement inspired by a deepseated mind-set which is also unique to the archipelago. This deals with the survival instinct and a physical and psychological need to possess a highly practical fighting art. For example, those of an indigenous group called the Dayak in Kalimantan province on Borneo were famed headhunters. Their trophies remind us that the origin and purpose of martial arts were focused on life and death realities of combat. Such arts are not practiced for sport and will never gain great popularity.

As author, I can only write from my own experience with kuntao-silat. Here we looked briefly at the teachings of Willem Reeders as viewed through my studies with Arthur Sykes and Richard Lopez, contacts with others familiar with Reeders, and with some supporting published books and articles dealing with kuntao-silat.

It is apparent that Reeders and many Indonesian martial art masters studied with a variety of teachers and mixed styles into their own hybrid systems. The de Thouars brothers certainly did this too.

Most martial art systems are not as neatly organized with detailed lineage scrolls as those found in Japan. On the contrary, it seems most combative arts have developed ad hoc, infused by experts through fateful circumstances. Generally, Indonesian kuntao-silat systems do not have reliable documentation for their history and evolution. It would be interesting and insightful to have access to details regarding family histories, lineages, reports on how kuntao-silat was utilized over the centuries, and precise overviews of all physical and mental practices associated with particular systems. However, many details are not necessary. What does the art itself exhibit? Effectiveness is the only yardstick for measuring a truly combative system.

In the case of kuntao-silat, we can see and feel the highly effective fighting techniques in the many styles found in Indonesia. We can learn more about the individual styles: Cimande, Pencak Silat, Bakti Negara, Cikalong, Harimau, Serak, etc. Learning even a little about such arts will certainly prove insightful for those practicing and researching other Asian styles that have either lost their original combative foundations or have focused on other aspects, such as health, sport, or entertainment.

In addition to its near-mystic mental states, distinguishing traits of kuntao-silat can be seen in its beautiful, dancelike fluidity of movement; human imitation of animal stances accompanied by panther clawing, gorilla striking, evasive monkey stepping, and snake-darting finger strikes. All such traits organically combine in kuntao-s to embody radar sensitivity to spontaneously face any realistic combative situation.

Acknowledgment
Special thanks to Rick Von Kaenel for posing for the technical section and Amanda Montgomery for photography; and to Richard Lopez for his teachings and friendship over the decades.

Bibliography

Alexander, H., Chambers, Q., & Draeger, D. (1974). *Pentjak-silat: The Indonesian fighting art*. Tokyo: Kodansha International Ltd.

Chambers, Q., & Draeger, D. (1979). *Javanese silat: The fighting art of Perisai Diri*. Tokyo: Kodansha International Ltd.

Cordes, H. (1990). *Pencak silat: Die kampfkunst der Minangkabau und ihr kulturelles umfeld*. Ph.D. dissertation, University of Cologne, Germany.

Davies, P. (2000). Kuntao: Cultural marginality in Indo-Malay martial tradition. *Journal of Asian Martial Arts*, 9(2), 28–47.

Dohrenwend, R. (2002). The odd East Asian sai. *Journal of Asian Martial Arts*, 11(3), 8–29.

Draeger, D. (1972). *The weapons and fighting arts of Indonesia*. Rutland, VT: Tuttle Publishing.

Draeger, D., & Smith, R. (1969). *Comprehensive Asian fighting arts*. New York: Kodansha America.

Farrer, D. (2009). *Shadows of the prophet: Martial arts and Sufi mysticism*. Berlin, Germany: Springer.

Maliszewski, M. (1992). Meditative-religious traditions of fighting arts and martial ways. *Journal of Asian Martial Arts*, 1(3), 1–104. See subheading on "Indonesia," pages 26–29.

Maliszewski, M. (1990). Personal videotape recordings taken through Asia, including Indonesia.

Parker, C. (1995). Introduction to the welcoming postures of pencak silat. *Journal of Asian Martial Arts*, 4(4), 84–101.

Pauka, K. (2003). Silat-based Randai theater of West Sumatra makes its U.S. debut. *Journal of Asian Martial Arts*, 12(1), 48–65.

Pauka, K. (1999). *Randai and silek: Folk theatre and martial arts of the Minangkabau in West Sumatra*. CD-ROM. University of Michigan Press.

Pauka, K. (1998). *Theater and martial arts in West Sumatra: Randai and silek of the Minangkabau*. Ohio University Press.

Pauka, K. (1997). Silek: The martial arts of the Minangkabau in West Sumatra. *Journal of Asian Martial Arts*, 6(1), 62–79.

Pauka, K. (1996). A flower of martial arts: The Randai folk theatre of the Minangkabau in West Sumatra. *Journal of Asian Martial Arts*, 6(4), 10–29.

Pauka, K. (1995). Martial arts, magic, and male bonding: The pauleh tinggi ceremony in West Sumatra. *Journal of Asian Martial Arts*, 4(3), 26–45.

Wilson, J. (1993). Chasing the magic: Mysticism and the martial arts on the island of Java. *Journal of Asian Martial Arts*, 2(2), 10–43.

Opening and Closing:
Welcoming Postures of Pencak Silat
by Chris Parker, B.Ed.

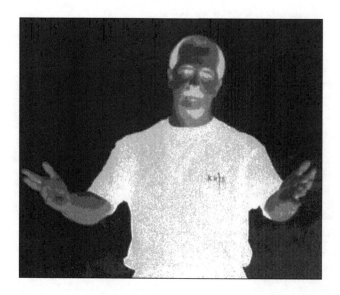

Increasingly, it seems, karateka are expressing an interest in analyzing the minute details of the kata they practice and the applications the kata contain. They should not be alone. An understanding of movement is something for which all martial artists should strive. In combat, two or more opposing forces fill a particular time and space: the victor is invariably the one who manages those two elements most successfully. Understanding the various applications of a specific movement, the rhythm(s) that can be achieved when employing it, and the space that it fills is of crucial importance, therefore, in achieving combative success and ensuring that the movements-kata, forms, patterns, etc.—are practiced with the appropriate attitude.

In the final analysis, of course, every movement that a person can make has myriad combative applications. We should not, therefore, restrict our study only to those movements that have been codified and left for us by previous masters. A martial art, by definition, should combine two elements: the warlike and the creative. As martial artists we should not want to fight; neither should we let our strengths blind us to the infinitely greater forces that exist around us. Perhaps the greatest challenge we face is to develop strength and humility in proportion, but we should be able to fight. We should possess that understanding of movement and mentality that enables us to fill time and space in a martial manner. Attitude is, arguably, the warrior's primary weapon. Knowledge of numerous applications is almost worthless if not driven by the appropriate mental state. Movements should create psychological states within us in a manner akin to the way an actor's state changes from role to role. We are performers too, even if our performance is sometimes a violent one.

However, it is not enough just to be able to fight, to have the ability to apply those movements handed down to us. As artists, we have an obligation to be creative. I am not suggesting that we should spend several months studying different arts, put them together to form an ad-hoc system, advertise ourselves as masters, and see how much money we can make from a gullible public! That might be a creative approach to the acquisition of wealth, but it is not the creativity of the serious martial artist. That creativity is based on an ever-increasing understanding of movement. It is the ability to respond and feel in a way that is uniquely our own, to apply the same movement in different ways, at different ranges, using different rhythms and, perhaps, different mental states. At its highest level, martial creativity is the ability to let go of our preconceptions, negative beliefs and mind sets and become one with the movement. It is the time when we express ourselves rather than copying the routine of another, when the movement reveals the performer rather than the other way around. Of course, we need a structure, but it should be viewed as the foundation from which we build and to which we return, not as a prison that restricts our growth.

Neither should our creative understanding be limited only to the movements we practice. Every art contains a variety of postures—standing, sitting, lying positions-from which movements spring. These positions also contain a wealth of hidden meaning, limited only by the practitioner's awareness and imagination. It is the interpretation of some basic postures from the Malaysia art of pencak silat that is the focus of this article.

Let it be stressed that this is not intended as a definitive work or purely as a statement of the combat efficacy of the art. As a student of pencak silat for almost twenty years, I have noticed many changes in the public representation of the art. I was initially inspired to study pencak silat by a man rather than the art itself. After all, the value of any art form is determined by the qualities of its performers: an art exists only through the behavior, beliefs, and practices of its practitioners. Pencak silat is no different in this respect. In 1975, when I first was introduced to pencak silat, I had only seen one magazine article on the art. Now it is a common subject and too often, I feel, it is presented simply as the "deadliest martial art." While there can be no doubting that a practical understanding of the movements and mentality of silat does provide the student with a potent fighting ability, there is far more to the art than the development of destructive capabilities. It takes only a second to destroy, but a lifetime to create. An art that does not prepare us for the challenges of a lifetime leaves us vulnerable and unbalanced. So, the photos that accompany this piece are simply a reflection of my current understanding of the art. They will, hopefully, highlight certain points made which can offer insights into the art.

Opening and Closing

The patterns of pencak silat are sometimes referred to as a "flower dance" (*silat bunga*) and, at first glance, it would be easy to dismiss them as a simple dance form with no combative significance. The movements can appear light, delicate even, and are often performed to music. The hands are often kept open, performing graceful, flowing patterns through the air, and the postures are not overtly aggressive.

A more careful examination would lead to the realization that the movements encompass empty-hand and weapon techniques with little, if any, change of form. While the postures can be used to confuse and distract an opponent or lead him into a trap, they can be percussive techniques in their own right! They also play an integral part in helping the performer develop appropriate mind sets.

Some of the postures are open, revealing the centerline and, apparently, placing the practitioner in a position of weakness and vulnerability. Compared to the fighting stances of many other systems, in which the hands are raised in front of the chest or face to both threaten an opponent and act as barriers against a potential attack (Western boxing is an excellent example of this approach), the opening postures of pencak silat appear welcoming in nature. They do not say, "I am ready to repel your assault," but rather they invite the attacker in. They offer an opening, feign a weakness, and encourage the assailant to take the bait. Through their use, the silat practitioner aims to take control of the combat from the very beginning. If the opponent feels that he or she is actually in control, so much the better, but in reality, they are being led into a trap. The line of attack and sometimes the technique used have been determined for them. Their confidence in a quick and easy victory might well turn into panic once the first contact has been made and the flaw of their strategyhas been exposed.

Such opening postures require a certain mentality and reflect a certain philosophy. To feign weakness, to deliberately increase an opponent's confidence rather than work to diminish it, requires a very obvious degree of selfconfidence. Too often in the West we want people to recognize and be impressed by our strength from the outset of a relationship. Ours is not a culture that recognizes the value of hiding or disguising power. We want our strength to be seen, even at first glance. In silat, physical and mental postures can be assumed that are intended to dissuade an aggressor, but there is also an appreciation of the fact that an over-confident enemy who has failed to determine your combative capability is more vulnerable and likely to make an error than one who fears and respects your obvious power. I think it is fair to say that deceit and humility are two key attitudes in the mind and heart of a pencak silat practitioner.

The use of deceit increases our chances of winning a fight and reminds us that, in real combat, there are no rules. It also reinforces the principle that neither

92

situations nor people should be judged too quickly—things are not always as they seem—and the only defense against a surprise attack is not to be taken by surprise in the first place. The fact that the combative meanings of the postures are not easily discernible enables practitioners to "dance the dance" without revealing their significance to interested onlookers. The element of surprise is, therefore, maintained should an observer ever become an opponent. Humility is achieved through an awareness that the power of man, no matter how great, is transitory and limited.

The more open postures also reflect a willingness to accept life's problems and difficulties and to learn from the experience of dealing with them. Challenges and conflicts of one kind or another are unavoidable. They cannot always be avoided or warded off by an aggressive defense. So, the student of silat learns to welcome the challenges that life sends with open arms, regarding them as opportunities for growth, while at the same time trying to control and direct them from the earliest opportunity.

Many of the fighting postures in which the practitioner positions himself either very low to the ground or on the ground are unique to pencak silat and are emphasized in varying degrees by the various styles. While they share the practicality and adaptability of their upright counterparts and add the ability to fight on the ground to the practitioner's combative arsenal, they also help develop a "never-say-die" mentality. To the silat student, being on the ground does not equate with being out of the fight. It is not necessarily a sign of weakness or defeat. On a philosophical level, the postures can be used to remind us that even when we are knocked flat, either physically or emotionally, there is still room for maneuver. We are not in unknown territory; we know how to fight from here, so we will regroup in order to rejoin the fray.

Of course, not all postures in pencak silat appear open and vulnerable. However, those that do share a common response to an enemy's attack. They snap shut! The groin, stomach, throat, those targets that seem so accessible, are suddenly no longer there, and the counter-attack will often include close range techniques delivered to limbs and torso that would, if carried through their conclusion, cause serious injury and possibly death. This emphasis on what might be termed "overkill" has several benefits. It teaches the student to keep going if the first blow is unsuccessful. It develops the ability to fight from various angles, ranges, and positions—not all fights begin with the two combatants squaring up to each other—and to move comfortably from upright to ground fighting and vice versa. And it also creates an awareness of the potentially lethal consequences of combat, an awareness that should discourage all but the most hot-headed from rushing willingly into a fight. In other words, it decreases the likelihood of battle rather than increasing it.

Pencak Silat Technical Section

1a A classical "opening" posture inviting an opponent to attack to the centerline.

1b The same posture as *1a* but modified for a street situation. It is a non-threatening position, almost a conciliatory pose, which nevertheless allows for an immediate response and, again, is designed to direct the opponent's attach.

2a Another classical position in which the face and groin appear vulnerable.

2b The same posture as *2a* but modified for a street confrontation. The face and groin still appear vunerable, but the defender is prepared to receive attacks to these targets and his hands are positioned ready to counter-attack.

3a A typical low posture from which the practitioner can spring upright or drop lower still.

3b A change in body position, a slight shift in weight and a more aggressive mentality allow for a myriad of applications.

3c In this instance, the practitioner "drops" lower.

3d A basic interpretation of this move would be to drop underneath an attack and counter to the opponent's groin

Some other possible applications of this low stance and the two opening positions shown are explored in the following sequences.

4a The defender opens his arms, "preparing the way" for the attacker, encouraging a punch to the face. This is the posture shown in *1b*.

4b The attacker's punch is directed across his own body, hindering the delivery of a second blow. The defender combines this with a foot-pin and a head control maneuver.

4c The attacker's head is twisted and an elbow strike is delivered to the temple. By maintaining the foot-pin, the stress on the attacker's back and hips is increased. The defender's aim is, at all times, to hit and/or unbalance on every contact while maintaining control of his opponent's limbs and moving into a safe space—the place which allows him access to continue his defense, but which limits the attacker's options.

4d The attacker's head is driven down onto the defender's knee and a second elbow strike is delivered. This can be seen as one interpretation of the posture shown in *2a*.

4e The attacker is driven to the floor and a double-knee strike is combined with an arm-break.

4f While maintaining the arm-break, the defender assumes a version of the posture shown in *3a* using his foot to perform a neck wrench.

5a As for **4a**.

5b The attacker throws a right cross.

5c The defender moves forwards, trapping the punching arm and delivering a palm-heel strike to the jaw.

5d The defender continues his forward momentum, forcing the attacker back over his front knee.

5e The attacker's head is forced behind the defender's lead leg. The defender's rear knee is driven into the attacker's lower back to aid in the movement.

5f The defender drops into a version of the posture shown in *3c*. The defender's front leg strikes into the attacker's throat and serves to pin and control the attacker's arm. The defender's knee maintains its pressure on the lower back, forcing the attacker to arc his back slightly thus stretching his rib cage and presenting it as a vulnerable target for the defender's elbow strike.

5g The defender performs a heel-kick, knee-strike combination, simultaneously hitting the attacker's stomach and spine. An arm-break is also applied.

6a and **6b** as in *4a* and *4b*.

6c The defender crashes through the punch, knocking the punching arm down while delivering a forearm strike to the neck.

6d and **6e** The defender moves the attacker's head through 180 degrees and delivers an elbow strike.

6f The defender again drops into a version of the posture shown in *3c*. This time his lead leg is beneath the attacker's head, causing stress to his neck on impact. Both of the attackers' arms are controlled and an elbow strike is delivered to the face.

6g The defender then straightens, maintaining his control of the attacker's arms and delivers a heel-kick to the stomach.

6h and **6I** The kicking foot is then forced against the attacker's face, creating a neck wrench before twisting him away. A follow-up heel-kick is aimed at the lower ribs.

6j A version of the posture shown in *3a* becomes the defender's "escape" position.

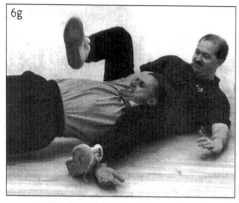

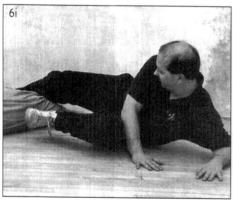

7a The attacker's left jab is forced across his body, preventing a second punch. At the same time, the defender performs an eye gouge and a knee strike to his opponent's leading knee.

7b The attacker's head is twisted and jerked back slightly. An elbow strike is delivered to the spine, while the pressure on his leading leg is increased.

7c The defender steps across from his right to left, to generate greater power in the elbow strike. At the same time, an arm wrench is applied and now his right shin strikes the attacker's already damaged leg.

7d Changing body position again, the defender's right knee strikes down onto the attacker's ankle. The defender's chest is used to strike the attacker's exposed elbow and his head is twisted and jerked back.

7e The attack to his ankle forces the attacker to the floor. The arm wrench is maintained and another elbow strike is delivered.

7f The defender drops back and drives the back of the attacker's neck onto his upraised knee. This position can be seen as another variation of the posture shown in *3c*, the difference now being that the knee is raised, rather than on the ground.

7g The defender lowers his leg and wraps it around the attacker's throat to create a neck wrench and choke. Again, the defender's limbs are monitored and controlled, and the defender can apply another wrench or an elbow strike.

8a The attacker throws a left jab. The defender parries the punch and scoops it down, while threatening the attacker's eyes as he moves in.

8b The defender steps to the outside of the attacker, but is then forced down and back over the defender's leading leg.

8c The defender drops into a version of the position shown in *3c*, the aim being to drive the back of the attacker's neck onto his knee. An elbow strike is delivered to the throat or face.

8d The defender leans away, straightens his right leg and brings it across the attacker's throat to create a neck choke and wrench. Control of the attacker's nearest arm is maintained.

8e and **8f** The defender rolls his hips, twisting the attacker over onto his stomach, where both arms are still held in check, thus allowing an elbow strike to be delivered to the spine. This is another possible application of the position shown in *3c*.

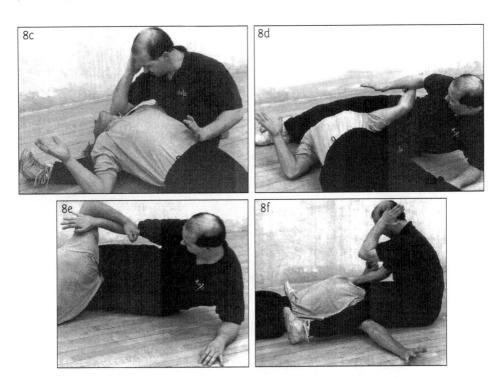

9a The attacker succeeds in grabbing the defender in a bear hug.

9b The defender drives off his right foot, simultaneously widening his stance, striking with his right knee to the outside of the attacker's knee, and flaring his elbows up and out.

9c and **9d** With the attacker unbalanced, the defender drives his knee down and assumes a version of the posture shown in *3a*. The attacker's knee is pinned beneath the defender's knee. The defender has control of the attacker's arms and continues his defense with a head butt.

9e The attacker is knocked back. The defender traps his nearest leg using another variation of the position shown in *3c* and delivers an elbow strike to the thigh.

10a The attacker threatens with a knife. He does not see the defender's knife. The defender's opening posture is a version of that shown in *1b*.

10b The attacker thrusts to the defender's face. The defender angles to the outside of the attack, simultaneously cutting the attacker's bicep and parrying the forearm. He then strikes the attacker's jaw or throat with the butt of the knife.

10c The defender wraps his arm around the attacker's, cutting the elbow and wrenching the arm to ensure that the knife will be dropped. He also applies a foot-pin and a head-control.

10d The defender slashes the attacker's stomach and thrusts into his groin, while forcing his opponent's back down and onto his knees.

10e The defender drops into a version of the position shown in *3c*. A forearm strike is delivered to the attacker's throat, and the groin or inner thigh are targets for another attack with the knife if required.

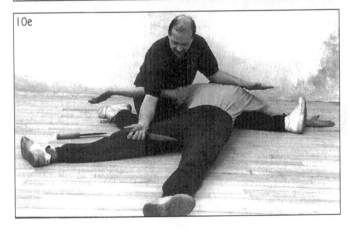

index

boilerplate
26261642R00065

Made in the USA
San Bernardino, CA
23 November 2015